A Miscellany of GARLIC

From Paying Off Pyramids and
Scaring Away Tigers to Inspiring Courage and
Curing Hiccups, the Unusual Power Behind the
World's Most Humble Vegetable

TRINA CLICKNER

Avon, Massachusetts

Published by
Adams Media, a division of F+W Media, Inc.
57 Littlefield Street, Avon, MA 02322. U.S.A.
www.adamsmedia.com

ISBN 10: 1-4405-2982-5
ISBN 13: 978-1-4405-2982-5
eISBN 10: 1-4405-3298-2
eISBN 13: 978-1-4405-3298-6

Printed in the United States of America.

10   9   8   7   6   5   4   3   2   1

Library of Congress Cataloging-in-Publication Data
is available from the publisher.

This publication is designed to provide accurate and authoritative information with regard to the subject matter covered. It is sold with the understanding that the publisher is not engaged in rendering legal, accounting, or other professional advice. If legal advice or other expert assistance is required, the services of a competent professional person should be sought.
—From a *Declaration of Principles* jointly adopted by a Committee of the American Bar Association and a Committee of Publishers and Associations

Many of the designations used by manufacturers and sellers to distinguish their product are claimed as trademarks. Where those designations appear in this book and Adams Media was aware of a trademark claim, the designations have been printed with initial capital letters.

"The Garlic Waltz," on pages 122–123, is reprinted with permission. Words and music by Rutthy Taubb, copyright © 1979 Chakra Troops Music. All rights reserved.

Figures on pages 11 and 15 are from *Growing Great Garlic: The Definitive Guide for Organic Gardeners and Small Farmers* by Ron L. Engeland. Okanogan, WA: Filaree Productions, 1991. Used with permission.

This book is available at quantity discounts for bulk purchases.
For information, please call 1-800-289-0963.

CONTENTS

DEDICATION

This book is dedicated to best friends, and, in particular, to my mother Elise and her very best friend Harmony—two magnificent moms, two unforgettable ladies.

ACKNOWLEDGMENTS

I have always believed that the solution to practically everything is within my reach and that the answer needed is right there in front of me, awaiting my notice. In other words, spoken in the language of the mobile computing techno pioneer that has defined me now for well over two decades, the answer is literally right in the palm of my hand.

The opportunity of this project, *A Miscellany of Garlic*, and garlic—the "super bulb" itself—have thankfully reinforced this fundamental belief at a time when I needed some reminding.

Heartfelt thanks go to my dear friends who are steadfast sources of encouragement no matter what expedition I embark upon. Even the burliest of my men friends have surprisingly admitted to exploring garlic remedies. The fact that even these manly men are willing to share their garlic experiments and experiences so openly with others amazes me. I thank you for sharing your stories and your "it's worked for me" testimonials. Anecdotal evidence—right in front of me. Again.

Thanks go to my parents, to my grandparents (both the exciting set and the boring set), and my aunt "Uncle Chrissy" who collectively saw to it that I was armed with a good education, confidence, tenacity, and now a fiddle and a published book on garlic. Thank you for leading by example simply by living your eclectic lives—it has allowed me the freedom to create my own professional path, to become an independent spinster with two basset hounds who believes in the possibilities of the nontraditional, the mystical, and the magical. And now garlic, too!

Thank you brother Todd for sharing your family garlic memories with me. I am still stunned that you remember Mom's safe garlic handling methods and I don't. I also missed that garlic clove as lozenge remedy for sore throats and colds, so what's up with that? Why have I always thought that I was the only one paying attention at the family table?

And, overall, thank you, Internet—you are so powerful, and young, and awesome. Sometimes you are really full of it, but like a decent, entertaining friend, I can't imagine my life today without you. You have brought so many opportunities my way and have allowed me to meet so many great people. I am very grateful.

A huge thanks to the public libraries right here in delightful Dunedin, Florida and Rochester, New York. Old-fashioned, printed books inspire me. Special thanks to libraries everywhere for making it easy to find perfect publications and then have them delivered to my neighborhood library branch with a simple click of the "request it" button. Books right at my fingertips. Now *that* was easy.

A final thank you to the garlic gurus, growers, and greats mentioned throughout this book. Thank you for taking the time to share your knowledge, resources, lyrics, drawings, tasting notes, and even your garlic crops with me. And thank you for being so enthusiastic about this book and about garlic.

INTRODUCTION

It has been used for everything from currency to a remedy for hiccups. In its hundreds of varieties it has been an essential part of world culture for 10,000 years. Ancient humans, huddled around their campfires in caves, bundled in bear skins knew of its properties. Today, chefs in kitchens gleaming with stainless steel appliances wouldn't be caught without it. In shops from Verona to Mexico City to Beijing, it dangles in long white and purple braids.

Its Latin name is *allium sativum*. You know it as common garlic. But there's nothing common about it.

Curious, isn't it, that such a humble vegetable—a cousin of the onion, one nicknamed "the stinking rose"—should be so pervasive? And yet there's hardly a day that goes by in which you don't encounter it. Often, of course, you meet it in food; it's the most common flavoring agent in the United States, beat out only by pepper. We find it in the food we buy for ourselves and our pets. It's in soup, salad dressing, mustard, and chips.

Yet throughout history we've found other ways to employ it. We've used it as a health remedy, a mosquito repellent, a glue for binding porcelain and paper, a laxative, and an aphrodisiac. Garlands of it were hung over the cradles of newborns to protect them from evil spirits.

Not surprisingly, garlic is widely represented in the world's art. Great painters such as Velazquez and Van Gogh put it in their pictures. A movie has been made about it, and it appears in poems and songs.

Its storied powers include repelling vampires and witches and preventing the spread of the Black Death during the Middle Ages. In modern times it's been the basis of physical therapy. In the 1960s, Americans rediscovered garlic (along with much else) as a flavoring ingredient through the great Julia Child and her magnum opus, *Mastering the Art of French Cooking.*

Above all, garlic is something we're passionate about. That's true of no other vegetable. The world, in my experience, is divided into garlicphobes and those who love its acrid aroma and sharp, biting taste. Virtually no one, though, is indifferent to it.

Just ask some of the thousands of people who, every year, pour into the little town of Gilroy, CA, for the annual garlic festival. Those wandering the fairgrounds consume everything from garlic fries to garlic-flavored ice cream. They cheer on the contest to crown Miss Gilroy Garlic. Their devotion to this strange, unassuming little packet of flavor might be funny . . . if it weren't echoed by so many of us.

This book is a random collection of information about garlic. But it's more than that. It's a celebration, a reflection of our extraordinary love affair with this, the humblest of vegetables.

Enjoy!

CHAPTER 1

GARLIC 101

It's a Bird! It's a Plane! It's Super Bulb!

Some foods provide more than just nourishment and garlic is one of the super foods in this particular category. Garlic is more than edible—it's nature's most powerful, versatile, and flavorful healer. Garlic has earned the distinguished honor of being referred to as the "super bulb" because of its medicinal powers. Since 3000 B.C.E. it has been cultivated and used worldwide to heal the body, to ease the mind, to ward off pesky vermin, and to protect against evils of all kinds.

Powerful, Herbal, Healing Vegetable

Garlic is often heralded as an ancient, magical, healing herb. Magical, healing, and ancient it is indeed—and much more. But the fact is that garlic, which is used in herbal medicines around the world, is not really an herb at all. Garlic is a vegetable. But it is no ordinary vegetable.

Garlic is a powerful, natural antibiotic. It inhibits bacteria, lowers blood pressure, aids in digestion, and keeps plaque from building up in the arteries.

Back to Basics

Garlic is a tenacious, biennial bulb vegetable that is easy to grow and adapts well to practically any environment. It is designed to withstand cold and drought and is engineered by Mother Nature to survive—it endures all climates and is able to protect itself against natural assaults by hungry predators. For protection, both the bulb and the cloves are wrapped in paper-like skins, and garlic's inherent antibiotic and antifungal properties enable it to resist decay. Allicin, one of the powerful enzymes that garlic produces when it is cut or crushed, is a smelly, yet very successful self-defense mechanism and a key component of garlic's self-preservation strategy. Once a bug or beast bites into it, the strong taste and the severe smell say, simply and succinctly, "scram."

The garlic plant's long, flat leaves turn brown when the underground bulb, the most prized part of the plant that hides below the ground, is ready to harvest. Although both the garlic bulb and leaves are edible, the bulb is where the heat is once it is dried and cured.

Early in the garlic season, you may find "green garlic" or "garlic greens" at the farmers' market. These are immature garlic plants that can be used as salad greens or simply sautéed as a flavorful side dish.

Hardneck garlic produces flower stalks that twist and curl. These are called "scapes" and they can be snapped off and eaten when they are young. They add an earthy and exotic flair to salads and sautés and make growing hardneck garlic much more fun than softneck garlic because only hardnecks produce scapes.

When garlic is fresh out of the ground, the bulb is soft and very mild, tasting much like the earthy vegetable that it is. It is the curing process that hardens the bulb and brings out the full, sharp taste. Curing typically takes from four to six weeks (see Chapter 5, *Growing Your Own*).

Garlic is propagated by planting the cloves. That said, hardneck garlic "bolts" or produces flower stalks with seedpods and bulbils. Bulbils look like miniature garlic cloves and they can be planted to propagate garlic.

Hardneck or Softneck?

There are two main types of garlic—hardneck garlic and softneck garlic (see Chapter 5, *Varieties*). Hardneck garlic bolts, which means it produces a single flower stalk, also known as a scape. It is considered to be far tastier and "gourmet."

You can find hardneck garlic mainly at farmers' markets or you can order it online direct from growers listed in Chapter 6: *Garlic Getaways and Essential Resources* of this book. Organic farmers mainly choose to grow hardnecks because hardnecks are tastier and thus provide a successful niche market for small farmers. Softneck garlic is the more common, usually California-grown, garlic you'll find in your local grocery store.

There's Nothing Like Family

Refer to the *Allium Sativum* Family Tree and you'll see that garlic is a powerful and distinguished bulb vegetable that is a revered member of Family *Liliaceae*, the lily family, *Genus Allium*, the onion group. It is the strongest and boldest allium family member and is related to the other tasty alliums you may know: shallots, onions, leeks, scallions, and chives. These have all been relished across cultures since long before recorded history.

Allium Sativum Traditional Family Tree (based on USDA classification)

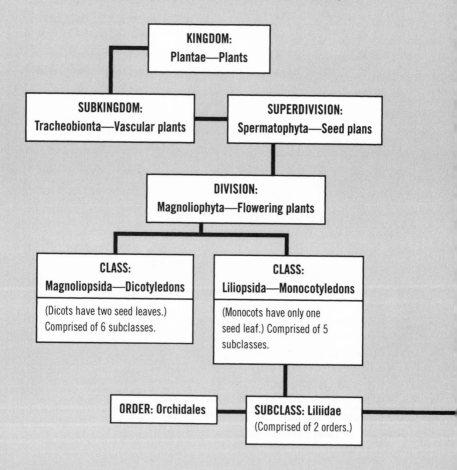

KINGDOM:
Plantae—Plants

SUBKINGDOM:
Tracheobionta—Vascular plants

SUPERDIVISION:
Spermatophyta—Seed plans

DIVISION:
Magnoliophyta—Flowering plants

CLASS:
Magnoliopsida—Dicotyledons

(Dicots have two seed leaves.)
Comprised of 6 subclasses.

CLASS:
Liliopsida—Monocotyledons

(Monocots have only one
seed leaf.) Comprised of 5
subclasses.

ORDER: Orchidales

SUBCLASS: Liliidae
(Comprised of 2 orders.)

ORDER: Liliales
(Comprised of the 12 families listed below.)

Agavaceae (Century plant)
Aloaceae (Aloe)
Dioscoreaceae (Yam)
Haemodoraceae (Bloodwart)
Hanguanaceae (Hanguana)
Iridaceae (Iris)
Liliaceae (Lily)
Philydraceae (Philydraceae)
Pontederiaceae (Water-Hyacinth)
Smilacaceae (Catbriar)
Stemonaceae (Stemona)
Taccaceae (Tacca)

FAMILY: Liliaceae (Lily)
(Comprised of 108 genera; common genera are listed below.)

Agapanthus L'Hér (Agapanthus)
Allium (Onion)
Alstroemeria (Lily of the Incas)
Amaryllis (Amaryllis)
Asparagus (Asparagus)
Hemerocallis (Daylily)
Hyacinthus (Hyacinth)
Lilium (Lily)
Narcissus (Daffodil)
Trillium (Trillium)
Tulipa (Tulip)

GENUS: Allium (Onion)
(Comprised of 112 species; common, culinary species listed below.)

Allium ampeloprasum (Broadleaf wild leek, aka: elephant garlic)
Allium ascalonicum (Wild onion, aka: shallot)
Allium cepa (Garden onion)
Allium fistulosum (Welch onion, aka: scallion)
Allium odorum and Allium tuberosum (Chinese chives)
Allium porrum (Garden leek)
Allium sativum (Cultivated garlic)
Allium schoenoprasum (Chives, wild chives)
Allium trioccum (Ramp)

SPECIES: Allium Sativum (Cultivated Garlic)

Subspecies: Hardneck	Subspecies: Softneck
Rocambole	Artichoke
Purple Stripe	Silverskin
Marble Purple Stripe	
Glazed Purple Stripe	
Porcelain	
Asiatic	
Turban	
Creole	

Where Does Garlic Come From?

If you are inspired to investigate garlic more intimately, you will need to get your hands on hardneck garlic. We found it difficult to obtain locally in the timeframe we needed it for this book, but were thrilled to find it easy to order online, direct from some fantastic growers who also proved to be great sources of information for this book (see Chapter 6).

The fresh, grocery store garlic that most Americans are familiar with comes from California or Mexico, depending upon the time of year. If it's ordinary, pure white-skinned, sort-of-shiny garlic, chances are that it's a softneck from California and either an artichoke variety or a silverskin variety. If it's springtime and the garlic is purple and white with a dull finish, it's probably Mexican garlic that has made its way over the border just in time to replenish the old California bulbs that have begun to shrivel, shrink, sprout, and stink. The purple-skinned garlic tends to be milder in taste than other softneck artichoke garlics. (See *Varieties* in Chapter 5 for details.)

In the United States, garlic is grown commercially mainly in California, but also in Texas and Louisiana. The United States imports millions of pounds of fresh garlic annually from Argentina (January through March), and from Mexico (starting in April). Garlic is also imported from Chile, China, Spain, and Taiwan. Italy, Spain, and southern France are the primary garlic-growing regions in Europe.

Proven Health Benefits

Eating garlic has bolstered and prolonged the strength of historical powerhouses such as the Roman and Greek soldiers and the Egyptian pyramid builders. Used as a traditional folk medicine, garlic has cured toothaches, addressed intestinal ailments, and protected open wounds from infection. (See *Folk Remedies and Natural Cures* in Chapter 5.) Garlic has captured the modern world's attention, too, and has been scientifically proven to be a powerful natural healer that helps people with high blood pressure, heart disease, diabetes, and cancer. And garlic, a natural remedy, has fewer side effects than prescription medications.

Garlic Prevents and Reverses Heart Disease

▶ Garlic slows the liver's production of cholesterol.

▶ Garlic pushes fat from the body into the bloodstream for use or elimination.

▶ Garlic lowers cholesterol, triglycerides, and LDL.

▶ Garlic elevates HDL.

Garlic Reduces and Stabilizes Blood Pressure

▶ One of garlic's sulfur amino acids prevents angiotensin 1 from becoming angiotensin 2, resulting in lowering blood pressure.

▶ Garlic elevates low blood pressure.

Garlic Reduces the Chance of Stroke

▶ Garlic thins the blood and prevents blood clots from forming inside the body.

Garlic Fights Infection and Cancer

▶ Garlic stimulates the immune system's cancer-fighting activity.

▶ Garlic stimulates the body to trap and eliminate toxins.

▶ Garlic kills bacteria, yeast, viruses, parasites, and tumor cells.

Garlic Protects Against Harmful Toxins and Pollution

▸ Garlic traps and removes heavy metals, toxins, and cancer-causing agents from the body.

▸ Garlic enhances the liver's natural ability to detoxify.

Garlic Helps Regulate Blood Sugar

▸ Garlic helps the liver more effectively filter blood sugars.

▸ Garlic increases the body's natural production of insulin.

Garlic Helps You Achieve Weight-Loss Goals

▸ Garlic helps to regulate blood sugar and can reduce hunger pains, cravings, and binges.

▸ Garlic can reduce the body's production of fat.

▸ Garlic pushes fat from the body into the bloodstream for use or elimination.

▸ Garlic increases metabolism.

Garlic's healing powers are at their most powerful when the garlic is fresh, but there are many popular garlic supplements on the market that are effective, too, and some are odorless. See *Supplements* in Chapter 5.

Garlic in the Yard and Garden

Garlic can be used to make a garden spray to fend off both insects and disease. Garlic spray is an insecticide that kills aphids and other pesky bugs as well as an antibiotic that kills fungus on plants. Garlic also protects you and your pets from mosquitoes. "Companion planting" with garlic ensures neighboring plants are safe because garden pests stay away from garlic.

The Stinking Rose

Garlic gets a bum rap mainly because of its lingering smell. Allicin, one of the key, health-packing compounds produced by garlic when it is crushed or cut, is absorbed by the body, and then comes back out through the pores and the breath. Raw garlic makes you smell more than cooked garlic and the more garlic you eat, the more you exude garlic odor as you breathe and perspire. Garlic odor sticks with some people longer than others—individual chemistry and metabolism factor in. Everyone is affected differently.

Shhh! There's an Elephant in the Room!

Elephant garlic is really a leek in garlic garb. Elephant garlic is about the size of an orange, and although it's the biggest of the bunch in size, it is not the best choice if you're looking for big garlic taste. Because elephant garlic is a leek, it tastes like a leek and is quite mild. Botanically speaking, you'll be sure to find it on the grocery store shelf mistakenly misplaced among the garlics. It is almost never in the leek lineup.

The smell of garlic is supposed to be so powerful that if you rub a clove of garlic on your bare foot, you will be able to taste the garlic in your mouth and smell it on your breath within a few minutes. We tried this a few times with no success. But then we don't think we ever smell like garlic!

What's Garlic Look Like?

Once you've seen and examined garlic growing the first time, you'll be able to recognize it again right away. You will also probably be surprised as you begin to notice garlic growing in gardens right in your very own neighborhood.

Above the ground, garlic resembles skinny, pathetic-looking, wilting corn with no ears. It is sparse and stands no more than about three feet tall. In urban gardens, it's often the one crop that doesn't need a fence to protect it from late night critter pilfering because these persistent pests don't like the taste of it.

The following diagram details the anatomy of a rocambole garlic plant, a hardneck, scape-producing garlic. The diagram comes from *Growing Great Garlic* by Ron Engeland, a book that profiles garlic and how it grows in great detail. We'll cover only the basics here.

The Leaves (the Greens)

The leaves of a garlic plant are long, flat, tapered, and fairly thin. Depending upon the variety of garlic, plant leaves range from light green to blue-green. See *Varieties* in Chapter 5 where the noteworthy leaf coloring of specific garlic varieties is listed, where available. When a garlic plant is young, the leaves are tender enough to be eaten and the entire plant is uprooted and sold as "garlic greens" or "green garlic." The older the plant gets, the stiffer and more fibrous the leaves become, which makes them great for weaving into garlic braids but too tough to eat.

Garlic plants have leaves that are either fertile or non-fertile. Only fertile leaf sheaths produce layers of cloves.

THE ANATOMY OF THE GARLIC PLANT

Image reprinted with the permission of Filaree Garlic Farm.

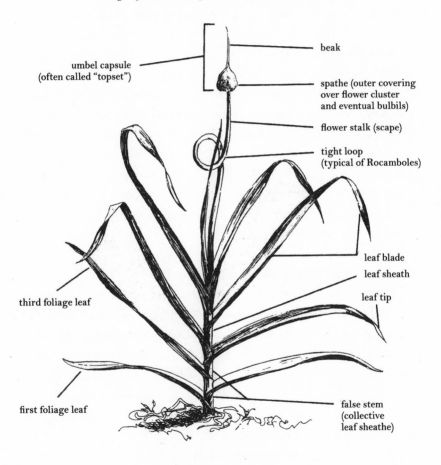

umbel capsule
(often called "topset")

beak

spathe (outer covering
over flower cluster
and eventual bulbils)

flower stalk (scape)

tight loop
(typical of Rocamboles)

leaf blade

leaf sheath

leaf tip

third foliage leaf

first foliage leaf

false stem
(collective
leaf sheathe)

**Allium sativum subspecies ophioscorodon
Variety Rocambole (typical)**

When most of the leaves turn brown and droop, the garlic bulb below ground is ready to harvest. See Chapter 5, *Growing Your Own*, for details that will help you determine when to harvest your own crop.

The Flower Stalk (the Scape)

Only hardneck garlic produces a flower stalk, or scape. Garlic that produces a flower stalk is said to have the "ability to scape." Although garlic produces one and only one scape, the shape of the scape gets crazy—it coils around in loops before it straightens itself out in the end. Scapes are often snapped off so that the garlic plant will focus all its energy underground to produce the biggest and best bulb possible. The scapes are often sold at farmers' markets and the middle segments are used for salad, sautés, and stir fries. Softneck garlic is infertile and does not bother with the fanfare of sending up a flower stalk.

The Umbel Capsule (the Seedpod)

Hardneck garlic tops off its scape with an exotic looking seedpod that contains flowers and tiny garlic bulbils. The bulbils look and smell just like miniature garlic cloves and can be planted, but it's the slow route on the garlic-growing road because bulbils take two or more years to produce a garlic bulb big enough to eat. Garlic is usually cultivated from cloves.

"A garlic caress is stimulating.
A garlic excess soporific."
—CURNONSKY (MAURICE EDMOND SAILLAND)

The Garlic Plant—Below Ground

Most of us purchase fresh garlic by the bulb and by the time it arrives home with us and is out the sack, it's a neat little package. To learn more about what your garlic goes through before you get it, see Chapter 5. Meanwhile, here's a quick look at the parts of garlic that grow quietly underground.

The Bulb (the Head)

The garlic bulb is also commonly called a head of garlic, and it is actually the plant's underground food storage area that it calls upon for nourishment. The garlic bulb is made up of individual garlic cloves that are organized in a circular pattern around the central stem.

In a typical rocambole hardneck garlic bulb, the center of the bulb is a flower stalk, which is surrounded by several separate clove layers. These are surrounded by thin, paper-like, inner bulb wrappers. Each clove layer and grouping is individually formed by the lower part of a single, fertile, foliage leaf.

On the other hand, a typical silverskin softneck garlic bulb is probably what's sitting in your kitchen. In this bulb, the five clove layers, and the wrapper that surrounds each layer, are produced by five distinct fertile leaves.

The whole arrangement of cloves is held firmly together to form the bulb by thin layers of paper-like skin that range in color from silvery, shiny white to matte purple depending upon the variety of garlic. Garlic bulbs range in size from about 1.5 inches in diameter up to 3 inches and usually have rounded bottoms with a flat spot in the middle where the roots have been trimmed.

The Clove (the Flesh)

Getting to the essence of it all, we arrive at the garlic clove, sometimes referred to as "flesh," particularly when cooked.

COOKING TIP

When cooking with garlic, be sure to read the recipe very carefully, distinguishing between "clove" and "bulb." Too often, hasty cooks read "Add a clove of garlic" as "Add a bulb of garlic." Eating spaghetti sauce to which an entire bulb of garlic has accidentally been added will probably keep your friends and family away from you for several weeks.

A garlic clove is really a plump leaf sheath that protects and feeds the garlic bud that's hidden inside the clove. Each garlic clove is individually protected by a single parchment paper-like wrapper that ranges in color from white to purple to bronze depending upon the variety of garlic.

The following diagram details the anatomy of a clove of garlic. The diagram comes from *Growing Great Garlic* by Ron Engeland, a book that profiles garlic and how it grows in great detail. It is used by permission. We'll cover only the basics here.

Clove size varies depending on the variety of garlic and typically measures .5 inch to 2 inches. Both clove size and how easily it peels depend upon freshness and the variety of garlic.

The Roots

Garlic roots come out of the base or basal plate of the bulb and serve to keep the bulb nourished and growing while it is underground. Garlic roots resemble big, stiff, crazy, wiry whiskers. Like chin hairs on a pretty girl, they are always removed before public appearances.

ANATOMY OF A GARLIC CLOVE

Image reprinted with the permission of Filaree Garlic Farm.

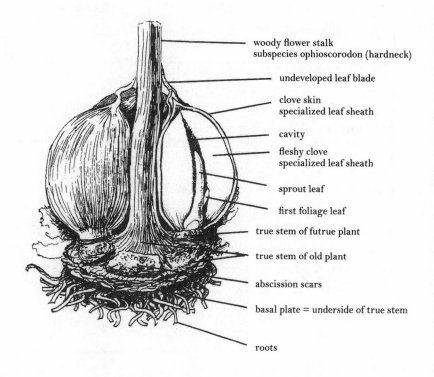

woody flower stalk
subspecies ophioscorodon (hardneck)

undeveloped leaf blade

clove skin
specialized leaf sheath

cavity

fleshy clove
specialized leaf sheath

sprout leaf

first foliage leaf

true stem of futrue plant

true stem of old plant

abscission scars

basal plate = underside of true stem

roots

Filaree Garlic Farm was founded by garlic great Ron Engeland, who also authored *Growing Great Garlic*, the bestselling
classic garlic-growing book among gardeners and farmers.
Be sure to visit Filaree Garlic Farm online at *www.filareefarm
.com* to purchase fresh garlic to eat, garlic gardening packs
to grow, and for garlic tips and resources of all kinds.

Chemistry—A-A-Action

What gives garlic its amazing ability to lower total cholesterol, curtail cardiovascular disease, and head off hardening of the arteries? It's all in the
chemistry that is unleashed when you crush or cut a clove. Here is a very
basic overview of the truly amazing way in which it happens. For a full scientific rundown and a whole lot more on garlic, grab a copy of *Garlic and
Other Alliums: The Lore and the Science* by Harvard University PhD, the great
garlic guru Dr. Eric Block. Chapter 4, "Chemistry in a Salad Bowl: Allium
Chemistry and Biochemistry," is for you.

Alliin

Alliin (S-allyl cysteine sulfoxide) is a garlic-specific amino acid that is void of both taste and smell. It lies dormant within the garlic clove until the clove is crushed or chopped, when it springs into action with alliinase to produce allicin.

Alliinase

Alliinase (S-alkyl-L-cysteine sulfoxide lyase) is an enzyme, or biological catalyst, that is made from protein present in garlic. Alliinase interacts with alliin and garlic's non-volatile components to create allicin plus many other medicinal, volatile sulfur compounds.

Allicin

Allicin (diallyl thiosulphinate) is produced only when garlic is chopped or crushed. Chopping or crushing garlic allows the alliin and alliinase to blend together to create allicin. This process takes about ten seconds. Allicin is the almighty, active, sharp, pungent, and medicinal component of garlic that is a natural insecticide and a powerful killer of bacteria. Allicin also combats mold, yeast, and viruses. Allicin degrades completely in about twenty-four hours. Its power is diminished by heat, but as it degrades, allicin produces more than two dozen new, powerful, sulfur-rich compounds that have tremendous medical benefits.

Diallyl Disulfide (DADS)

As it degrades, allicin produces diallyl disulfide (DADS). DADS is a powerful, sulfur-rich compound that has proven to slow cancer growth and to shrink tumors. DADS is not produced right away, however—it takes about fifteen to twenty minutes after a garlic clove is crushed. So if you are cooking with garlic and want to harness its maximum cancer-fighting capabilities, crush your cloves in a small bowl and let them sit for at least fifteen minutes while you prepare your other ingredients.

Selenium

Garlic contains trace amounts of selenium. Selenium is an antioxidant and helps to protect against aging, cancer, and heart disease. Selenium teams up with vitamin E for both heart and liver health, and to promote healthy skin and hair; it is important for fertility, growth, metabolism, and normal thyroid function.

I can't get enough garlic!

—TED WILLIAMS

CHAPTER 2

THE ANCIENT HISTORY OF GARLIC

Throughout history, garlic has been used in many ways and has played a prominent role across cultures, classes, and just about everywhere on earth. Garlic has been used as a powerful political pawn, a valuable currency, a potent medicine, a glue, a protector against evil, a preservative, a cover-up, a celebrated crop, and, of course, as a favorite food. It is a vegetable, a spice, a good luck charm, a power tool, and a pharmacy, all in one.

Have Garlic, Will Travel

Garlic is believed to have originated in southeast or central Asia and then carried by travelers throughout the rest of the world. Because garlic is mobile and stores well, it found its way easily into China, India, Egypt and the Middle East, and North Africa.

As garlic made its way across Asia it went through what is known as the Fertile Crescent, an agriculturally rich, arc-shaped area that follows the Euphrates and Tigris Rivers from the Persian Gulf to the Mediterranean Sea.

Garlic continued on to southern Europe and then traveled with Christopher Columbus across "the pond" to the Americas.

The fact that the word for garlic is very different in most languages around the world is an indication that once garlic arrived in an area, it adapted well and was cultivated locally.

Significant Events

The Timeline of Garlic lays out many specific and significant garlic-related events, providing an overview of many important moments in garlic history. Here are some other comments about garlic's role in ancient history:

A Working-Class Food

Throughout history, garlic—and the smell of garlic—has been associated with the peasant, laboring classes who relied on its powers for sustenance and health. Smell set people apart in the days when there were very few luxury items, such as perfume. The rich doused themselves in expensive scents; the poor smelled of what they flavored their food with—garlic. This peculiar prejudice persisted all the way into the late nineteenth and early twentieth centuries, when Italian immigrants to the United States were often contemptuously referred to as "garlic eaters."

Though the smell of garlic might indicate a person's low class, the status of garlic itself was never questioned when it came to medicine. Garlic was an esteemed and powerful natural healer that was used literally around the globe.

Do not eat garlic or onions; for their smell
will reveal that you are a peasant.
—CERVANTES, *DON QUIXOTE*

Garlic Built the Pyramids

The ancient Egyptians grew garlic and used it as a currency, power food, mummification method, and medicine. During the Old Kingdom (2650–2134 B.C.E.) a number of Egyptian rulers undertook to build huge pyramids as tombs and monuments to their magnificence. Garlic was used to compensate and to strengthen the pyramid-building teams. The pharaohs usually ensured their laborers had the food they needed to build the pyramids, but when garlic was withheld from the workers or was late to arrive, these workers threatened to strike.

Ancient Greek historian Herodotus (484–425 B.C.E.) documented an inscription on the Great Pyramid of Giza (tomb of the pharaoh Khufu) that tallied up the value of the garlic, onions, and radishes consumed by the Herculean, Egyptian laborers who were charged with building it. The grand total was 1,600 silver talents, an estimated $30 to $50 thousand.

Roman naturalist and author Pliny the Elder (C.E. 23–79) wrote that the Egyptians worshiped garlic and even swore on it when taking an oath.

Garlic remnants were found in many Egyptian tombs, even in King Tut's tomb. Onions and garlic were both prevalent in ancient Egyptian monument paintings as well. Egyptian wall paintings that date back to 2700 B.C.E. depict great feasts that included garlic and onions spread out at bountiful banquets and as offerings to the gods.

Let My Garlic Go!

The Egyptians got the Hebrews hooked on garlic as a power food. After exiting Egypt, the Land of the Pharaohs, the Hebrews went wandering in the wilderness for forty years in search of the Promised Land. The journey was long, they were tired and hungry and weak, and they needed and missed garlic. They had every reason to kvetch, and so they did. They complained directly to Moses.

"We remember the fish, which we did eat in Egypt freely; the cucumbers, and the melons, and the leeks, and the onions, and the garlic" (Numbers 11:5, King James version). It makes you wonder if, when the Lord sent them manna in the wilderness He remembered to include some garlic.

Sweet Garlic Love

The Talmud recommends eating garlic on Friday nights, the night of lovemaking or "marital bed."

The Ancient Greeks

The Greeks cannot lay claim to inventing or discovering garlic, but they have long used it for medicinal purposes and as a dietary staple. In grand, feasting fashion, the Greeks preferred to bake it and consume whole heads of it at one time. Garlic pumped up the athletes at the Olympic games and was believed to give Greek soldiers gumption. One can imagine the Spartans who held off the advancing Persian army at Thermopylae in 480 B.C.E. stuffing themselves with garlic before their last, heroic stand.

Garlic was widespread in Greece from the very beginning. Garlic was found on the island of Crete at the site of the earliest Greek civilizations. However, the gods were said to disdain it because of garlic breath.

Fighting Off Witches

During the time of the ancient Greek poet Homer, garlic was believed to offer protection from witches. In his epic poem *The Odyssey*, Homer tells how golden garlic saved Odysseus from the witch Circe during his wanderings.

Keeping Away Bad Plants

Garlic was considered to provide protection when picking poisonous plants. Greeks slathered themselves in garlic oil for personal protection as they gathered the roots and leaves of the poisonous hellebore plant to use in warfare. Once they arrived safely home, they made poisonous potions for prisoners and saved the leaves for chemical warfare. Using garlic oil once again for protection, the Greeks crushed and dumped huge quantities of hellebore leaves into the water supply of the city of Kirrah in 585 B.C.E. Once the city's water supply was poisoned by the leaves, the people became so weak that the city eventually surrendered.

Ancient Greek physician Hippocrates himself (460–377 B.C.E.) prescribed garlic for a number of minor ailments including constipation and swelling, and also as treatment for lung disease and uterine tumors.

Garlic is hot, laxative, and diuretic, good for the body, bad for the eyes, for if the body is compelled to great purging, the sight becomes weaker. It is laxative and diuretic because of its purgative character. It is weaker boiled than raw.

—HIPPOCRATES

Following in the footsteps of Hippocrates, Greek traveling physician and botanist Dioscorides (C.E. 40–90) prescribed garlic for many ailments including boils, coughs, lice, ulcers, toothache, and dog bites. Dioscorides authored the oldest major medical treatise in C.E. 64 and titled it *De Materia Medica*. It presented details about hundreds of uses for healing herbs and plants, and was the authoritative medical reference for more than 1,500 years.

Let food be your medicine and your medicine be your food.

—HIPPOCRATES

Et Tu, Garlic?

The Romans believed that garlic was so mighty that they assigned it to be the power vegetable of Mars, the Roman god of war. Roman soldiers gnawed on raw garlic to pump themselves up for battle.

The poet Virgil (70–19 B.C.E.) described farm workers and sailors on long voyages as having been bolstered by garlic. During the height of the Roman Empire, however, garlic became a food for the working class only, as rich Romans considered it too mundane for their tables, reinforcing its lower-class status.

After the fall of Rome, during the European Middle Ages, monks became the keepers of herbal and medicinal knowledge, including the healing powers of garlic. Garlic was an almost universal plant in monastic gardens. In later centuries, garlic found its way into royal gardens. Back in vogue, it was considered an essential part of a daily diet, for people of all classes.

The Ancient Chinese

Ancient Chinese records dating back to 2000 B.C.E. document the Chinese use of garlic. The ancient Chinese loved to eat garlic, and also believed that garlic purified water and prevented food poisoning from meat and fish that had not been stored or prepared properly. Marco Polo documented this in 1324 in *The Travels of Marco Polo.*

The Chinese harnessed garlic's antibiotic and anti-inflammatory properties to help treat dysentery, yeast infections, and earaches. They also used garlic to stop nosebleeds, to heal snake and bug bites, and for glue. Onions, garlic, and ginger continue to be the powerful three seasonings in Chinese cuisine even today.

Timeline of Garlicky Events

This timeline begins with a simple caveman and ends with the 2010 publication of an all-encompassing book that documents the complex, newly discovered science of garlic. It is intended to provide an introductory, cross-cultural, at-a-glance overview of garlic through the ages.

- **8000** B.C.E.

  CAVEMEN USE GARLIC

  Garlic remnants were found scattered on the floors of ancient caves, indicating that humans harvested and used garlic well over 10,000 years ago. Garlic—so easy to use, even a caveman can do it.

- **4004** B.C.E.

  GARLIC FOOTPRINTS EXITING THE GARDEN OF EDEN

  Christian and Muslim legends both have it that once Satan's malicious mission of deceptive, dirty deeds was done and the Fall of Man was accomplished, Satan exited the Garden of Eden, leaving two footprints as he fled. Garlic (*Allium satium*) is said to have sprung up from his left footprint, and onions (*Allium cepae*) from his right footprint. This is the earliest case of good coming from bad.

- ## 3750 B.C.E.
  ### GARLIC SCULPTURES IN EGYPTIAN TOMBS
  Life-like clay sculptures of whole garlic bulbs, as well as paintings of garlic on tomb walls, were discovered by archeologists in ancient tombs at El Mahasna, Egypt. These burial offerings and tomb adornments indicate that garlic was a highly esteemed, Egyptian essential.

- ## 2560 B.C.E.
  ### GARLIC POWERED PYRAMID BUILDERS
  Garlic was a highly prized essential nutrient that provided the ancient Egyptian pyramid builders with monumental strength, stamina, and legendary endurance. When deprived of their garlic rations, the laborers went on strike and refused to work until their garlic demands were met. Garlic was so important in building the pyramids that this fact is actually inscribed directly on the Great Pyramid of Cheops at Giza. Garlic was also used as currency in Egypt—7 kilograms (about 15.5 pounds) of garlic would purchase one healthy male slave.

- ## 2300 B.C.E.
  ### ALLIUM AFFINITY DOCUMENTED IN SUMERIAN CUNEIFORM TABLETS
  The Sumerians lived in southern Mesopotamia (now Iraq) and documented the use of garlic as a dietary staple as far back as 2300 B.C.E. They inscribed small clay tablets with cuneiform script (a style of writing using the ends of reed pressed into damp clay tablets) to preserve their history. Garlic (*Allium sativum*), leeks (*Allium porrum*), and onions (*Allium cepae*) were Sumerian staples—so important that their use was recorded in imperishable clay.

- **2000** B.C.E.

  ## GARLIC USED AS A PRESERVATIVE AND GLUE BY THE CHINESE

  Ancient Chinese records document the Chinese use of garlic in cooking and also as a food preservative. The Chinese used—and still use today—sticky garlic juice as a glue to bind paper, glass, and porcelain.

- **1500** B.C.E.

  ## EGYPTIAN *CODEX EBERS* ENUMERATES TWENTY-TWO GARLIC REMEDIES

  The *Codex Ebers*, named after archeologist George Ebers who discovered it in 1872, is an ancient Egyptian medical reference that presents hundreds of therapeutic remedies, twenty-two of which contain garlic. Thought to be the oldest medical reference in Western civilization, the *Codex Ebers* details proven remedies that had already been in use by the Egyptians for thousands of years.

- **1400** B.C.E.

  ## GARLIC USED BY THE GREEKS AT THE PALACE OF KNOSSOS, ISLAND OF CRETE

  Garlic was found during archeological digs on the Greek island of Crete at the palace of Knossos, often referred to as the birthplace of ancient Greek civilization. Ancient Greeks, known as Minoans, employed garlic—they considered it to be an essential food for warriors as both a strength and mood enhancer.

- **1325 B.C.E.**

GARLIC TUCKED IN KING TUTANKHAMUN'S TOMB

The tomb of Egypt's youngest king, King Tutankhamun (1334–1325 B.C.E.), was discovered and excavated in 1922 by tenacious English archaeologist Howard Carter. In addition to the world-renowned ornate, golden sarcophagus, King Tut's stunning and incredibly well-preserved tomb housed decorative boxes, jewelry, figurines, and the simple, everyday Egyptian items that would be needed in the afterlife. This included a few sofas and, of course, garlic!

- **776 B.C.E.**

GARLIC SUMMONS SUPER STRENGTH DURING FIRST OLYMPICS

Like the Egyptians, the ancient Greeks also believed that eating garlic garnered them Herculean strength, and Olympic athletes consumed garlic galore as a natural performance enhancer. No steroids necessary!

- **377 B.C.E.**

HIPPOCRATES TREATS LUNG DISEASE AND CANCER WITH GARLIC

Hippocrates (460–377 B.C.E.), a Greek physician commonly revered as the "Father of Medicine," prescribed raw garlic as a laxative, a diuretic, and as a treatment for lung disease. He prescribed garlic vapors to treat cervical cancer. Many of his teachings are still practiced in modern medicine today.

- **322** B.C.E.

ARISTOTLE'S APHRODISIAC—ALLIUM SATIVUM

Renowned Greek philosopher Aristotle (384–322 B.C.E.) included garlic in his list of recommended aphrodisiacs. He postulated that garlic was a health enhancer, that it promoted overall strength, and that it was effective against dog bites—it prevented transmission of the rabies virus.

- **70** B.C.E.

FIRST GARLIC IN VERSE BY VIRGIL

Virgil wrote the first poem that featured garlic. The Latin title of the poem, "Moretum" translates into English as "The Salad." It describes mashing garlic with herbs, salt, and cheese and forming it into a ball as a spread for crusty, homemade bread.

- C.E. **1**

THE SANSKRIT *CHARAKA-SAMHITA* PRESCRIBES GARLIC FOR HEART DISEASE AND ARTHRITIS

The *Charaka-Samhita* was an ancient, Sanskrit medical manuscript from the region now known as India. The *Charaka-Samhita* prescribes garlic, as well as onions, to remedy heart disease and to treat arthritis.

• 64

DIOSCORIDES DESCRIBES GARLIC CURES IN
DE MATERIA MEDICA

De Materia Medica, or *Regarding Medical Materials* in English, was written by Pedanius Dioscorides (40–90). This five-volume treatise contained drawings and descriptions of more than 500 plants having medicinal properties, and included both formulas and prescriptions. It prescribed garlic for colds, coughs, intestinal worms, as an artery cleanser, and as a cure for baldness. Even though he was Greek, Dioscorides worked directly for the Roman Emperor Nero as the Roman army's chief physician.

• 79

PLINY THE ELDER RECOMMENDS GARLIC FOR SIXTY-ONE AILMENTS

Gaius Pliny (23–79), also known as Pliny the Elder, a prolific Roman naturalist, compiled the voluminous encyclopedia of natural science entitled *Historia Naturalis* in Latin, or *Natural History* in English. In *Historia Naturalis*, Pliny prescribed garlic as a remedy to counter sixty-one medical issues including asthma, arthritis, and ulcers, as well as snake and scorpion bites. *Historia Naturalis* was a closely followed medical reference throughout Europe for thousands of years. A naturally curious fellow to the end, Pliny the Elder died of asphyxiation while investigating the eruption of Mount Vesuvius.

• 500

FRIDAY NIGHT GARLIC FOR HEBREWS

The Talmud, the ancient document that is the defining authority covering the laws and customs of Orthodox Jews worldwide, recommends that married couples eat garlic on the sixth day of the week, Friday, the formally prescribed night for lovemaking.

- **802**

CHARLEMAGNE ORDERS GARLIC IN MONASTERIES

Charlemagne (742–814), also known as Charles the Great, was both King of the Franks and the first Holy Roman Emperor. Charlemagne was also the first to formally catalog plants and to document how gardens should be planned and cared for. His *Capitulare de Villis Imperialibis* laid the groundwork for estate and monastery gardens of the Middle Ages. It included eighty-nine plants, most of which had medicinal qualities. Garlic (*Allium sativum*) was, of course, listed among them, as was wild garlic (*Allium ursinum*).

- **1100**

FRENCH GARLIC SOUP FOR COLDS AND COUGHS, A.K.A. AILÉE

French records dating back to the 1100s describe a garlic soup-like mixture that was made from almonds, garlic, breadcrumbs, and chicken broth. Ailée was not haute cuisine—it was consumed to prevent colds and coughs throughout the twelfth, thirteenth, and fourteen centuries.

- **1324**

GARLIC USE IN ASIA DOCUMENTED BY MARCO POLO

Famous, Italian-born explorer, trader, and great observer, Marco Polo (1254–1324), traveled extensively throughout Asia on business. Back home in Venice, he participated in the Venice-Genoa war and was captured and imprisoned in Genoa for two years. During his brief time behind bars, Polo wrote the book published as *The Travels of Marco Polo* in which he described how the Chinese used garlic as a flavor enhancer and a food preservative.

- ## 1347–1666

GARLIC GUARDS AGAINST DISEASE DURING THE GREAT PLAGUES

Garlic was a well-known guard against insidious infection and deadly disease during Europe's great plagues that spread across the continent in waves for centuries. The plague, which originated in Central Asia, was thought to have been spread by fleas riding around on rats and was more prevalent in poorer neighborhoods. The last of the plagues, The Great Plague of London (1665), claimed more than 70,000 victims in London alone. Doctors carried garlic cloves with them in their pockets to protect themselves and in their bags when they ministered to patients.

- ## 1492

CHRISTOPHER COLUMBUS INTRODUCES CULTIVATED GARLIC TO THE AMERICAS

Christopher Columbus (1451–1506) provisioned his ships for voyage with garlic to bolster his crew. Although Native Americans had already been using both wild garlic and wild onions, Columbus brought cultivated garlic and onions to the Americas.

- ## 1543

FIRST FORMAL PHYSIC GARDEN OPENS IN PISA, ITALY

Physic gardens, also known as apothecary gardens, grew garlic and many other plants expressly for educational and medicinal purposes. Physic gardens became popular during the Renaissance (1540–1620) and were often attached to monasteries and tended by monks. The first formal physic garden was opened in 1543 in Pisa, Italy and was associated with the University of Pisa.

- ## 1595

SHAKESPEARE BADMOUTHS GARLIC IN *A MIDSUMMER NIGHT'S DREAM*

Garlic even came into play for William Shakespeare (1564–1616), who mentioned garlic in *The Winter's Tale*, *Coriolanus*, and *Measure for Measure*, *King Henry IV*, and *A Midsummer Night's Dream*. England did not (and still largely does not) embrace garlic like the rest of Europe—eating garlic, and therefore garlic breath, were considered to be traits of the lower classes, a stigma that has maligned garlic for centuries.

Most dear actors, eat no onions nor garlic,
for we are to utter sweet breath.

—WILLIAM SHAKESPEARE, *A MIDSUMMER NIGHT'S DREAM*

- ## 1652

THE *COMPLETE HERBAL* PRAISES GARLIC

British botanist and physician Nicholas Culpeper (1616–1654) published the *Complete Herbal*, the first British publication that formally documented garlic as an acceptable and proven remedy for dog and snake bites, intestinal worms, ulcers, skin problems, and abscesses.

• 1858

LOUIS PASTEUR DISCOVERS THAT GARLIC KILLS BACTERIA

Although most people know him for what he did for milk, famous French chemist Louis Pasteur (1822–1895) was one of the founding fathers of microbiology and developed modern germ theory, laying the foundation for much of today's medicine. In 1858 Pasteur discovered and reported on the antibiotic properties of garlic.

There are two Italies . . . The one is the most sublime and lovely contemplation that can be conceived by the imagination of man; the other is the most degraded, disgusting, and odious. What do you think? Young women of rank actually eat—you will never guess what—garlick! Our poor friend Lord Byron is quite corrupted by living among these people, and in fact, is going on in a way not worthy of him.

—LETTER FROM PERCY BYSSHE SHELLEY, POET

• 1897

DEBUT OF COUNT DRACULA

Irish author Bram Stoker (1847–1912) gave vampires their first public voice in his novel *Dracula*, published in 1897. The book became a movie in 1931 and, since that time, there have been countless remakes. In all of them, garlic plays a prominent role as a specific defense against vampires, whether Dracula or his minions.

The Professor's actions were certainly odd . . . First he fastened up the windows and latched them securely. Next, taking a handful of the flowers, he rubbed them all over the sashes, as though to ensure that every whiff of air that might get in would be laden with the garlic smell. Then with the wisp he rubbed all over the jamb of the door, above, below, and at each side, and round the fireplace in the same way. It all seemed grotesque to me.

—BRAM STOKER, *DRACULA*

• 1961

JULIA CHILD *MASTERING THE ART OF FRENCH COOKING*, VOLUME ONE

With the publication of *Mastering the Art of French Cooking, Volume One* in 1961, Julia Child (1912–2004) introduced French cuisine, with its fresh and at the time exotic ingredients, i.e. garlic, to America. Child's TV show, *The French Chef*, was produced for Boston public television from 1963 to 1973 and reruns spanned decades, extending her culinary influence and her love of garlic and fresh herbs across generations.

• 1974

FLOW-LEBEN TREATMENT WITH GARLIC SHOWER UNVEILED

Flow-Leben Treatment, an extremely unusual garlic-based medical therapy that involves both whole body garlic showers and covering problem spots with grated garlic, was invented and administered in Japan by Yoshio Kato with tremendous success. Kato describes his work in detail in his book *Garlic: The Unknown Miracle Worker* and includes photographs of his specially designed Flow-Leben treatment shower.

• 1974

JAMES BEARD MAKES CHICKEN WITH FORTY CLOVES OF GARLIC

James Beard (1903–1985) shocked America into going for the garlic in 1974 when he introduced "Chicken with Forty Cloves of Garlic" as one of his signature dishes, derived from everyday cooking in Provençe, the southeastern region of France. Beard, an aspiring thespian, found his fame in food and successfully combined his two great passions—acting and eating—as host of the world's first televised food show in 1946.

The air of Provençe was particularly perfumed by the refined essence of this mystically attractive bulb.
—ALEXANDER DUMAS, AUTHOR

• 1979

GILROY GARLIC FESTIVAL

The Gilroy Garlic Festival was started in 1979 by Don Christopher, founder of Christopher Ranch, the largest grower, processor, packer, and shipper of garlic in the United States The Gilroy Garlic Festival is the premier garlic event in America, held annually at the end of July. In 2010, the festival attracted more than 97,000 attendees and featured top chefs, dancing, music, and a garlic cook-off and contest. Gilroy, known as the "Garlic Capital of the World," is located just thirty-five miles south of San Jose, California.

- **1980**

GARLIC IS AS GOOD AS TEN MOTHERS DOCUMENTARY FILM RELEASED

This now hard-to-get-your-hands-on documentary film, directed by Les Blank, covers the history, cultivation, and culinary use of garlic. Filmed on location at the Gilroy Garlic Festival and in Berkeley, California at Alice Waters's renowned Chez Panisse restaurant, *Garlic Is as Good as Ten Mothers* documents the "garlic revolution," which is said to have started in the 1960s thanks to renowned chefs Julia Child and James Beard. The film was selected by the U.S. Library of Congress in 2004 for preservation in the U.S. National Film Registry, which consists of only 550 titles as of 2010. Go garlic!

- **1991**

RON ENGELAND'S *GROWING GREAT GARLIC* PUBLISHED

Ron L. Engeland is a name that comes up again and again in garlic-growing publications. Engeland's ground-breaking book, *Growing Great Garlic: The Definitive Guide for Organic Gardeners and Small Farmers*, educated and empowered backyard garlic growers everywhere. It was the first publication to detail the many varieties of garlic, how they differ from one another, and how to grow them organically. Way to grow, Ron!

- **2008**

TED JORDAN MEREDITH AUTHORS *THE COMPLETE BOOK OF GARLIC*

Who knew that there are literally hundreds of varieties of garlic? *The Complete Book of Garlic* takes a look at garlic globally and shows how the different varieties are related, where they come from, how they taste, and where they grow best. See *Varieties* in Chapter 5 for details.

• 2010

ERIC BLOCK PUBLISHES *GARLIC AND OTHER ALLIUMS*

Garlic had long been recognized as a powerful healer, even though hardly anyone understood how it worked. *Garlic and Other Alliums: The Lore and the Science*, written by Dr. Eric Block and published by the Royal Society of Chemistry, explains it all. It covers all aspects of garlic including cultivation, literature, history, medicine, and very detailed chemistry. It is the culmination of Block's thirty-five years of Allium research and has instigated more than $5.5 million in garlic-related research grants.

A Cure for Garlic Breath?

"GILROY, Calif.—Kurt Svardal, president of the 2011 Gilroy Garlic Festival Association (*www.gilroygarlicfestival.com*), announced today an alliance with Scope Mouthwash that will eliminate the longtime bane of the internationally acclaimed summertime food and entertainment extravaganza . . .

"'We've entertained nearly 4 million guests in 32 years of service,' Svardal said. 'Despite our worldwide popularity, we are constantly admonished for returning otherwise happy visitors to society with "inappropriate breath." Solving this problem has been foremost on our agenda since the Gourmet Alley pyro chefs ignited their first flame in 1979.'

"Scope's newest technology convinced [Scope owner Procter & Gamble] that three days, 100,000 hearty appetites and 6,000 pounds of fresh California garlic would provide an effective demonstration."

—FROM A PRESS RELEASE FROM THE GILROY GARLIC FESTIVAL

CHAPTER 3

GARLIC ACROSS CULTURES AND AROUND THE WORLD

A Family Divided—By Garlic

It seems that no one is indifferent to garlic—you are either for it, or against it.

I grew up in upstate New York as a happy-go-lucky, good girl in a loving, Greek-American family of four. My mother's parents were industrious, kind-hearted, fabulous, feast-fixing Greeks direct from Bitola, which during my childhood was sometimes in Yugoslavia, sometimes in Greece, but is currently in the Republic of Macedonia. My maternal grandparents excited me. My father's parents were austere, reserved, frugal Scottish-Canadians who garnered great pleasure from saving just about anything, and I usually found them boring.

Thanks to my mother, Elise, we all enjoyed a weekly tradition of Sunday family dinners together for as long as I can remember. When it came to both people and food, it seemed the more the merrier. But when it came to seasonings and spicing things up, we were an extended family firmly divided along the line of, you guessed it—garlic. It became crystal clear to me very early on that even though garlic was not something everyone agreed upon, the most important thing was that we get together regularly over a huge feast with enough dishes to please everyone. And so we did, time and time again.

Around the world, food brings us together at the same time that it pushes us apart, particularly when it pertains to garlic. Only a few cultures today are not big on garlic—the Japanese, the Scandinavians, and, no surprise here, the British. Elsewhere, garlic is an essential part of cuisine.

Garlic Naysayers

Let's get the garlic naysayers out of the way first.

If you're an experienced international traveler, chances are you know how complicated it can be to find a place to eat at the time you desperately need to eat. It sounds like it should be easy enough, but that's usually not the case. The body clock says one thing, the local time is GMT plus or minus whatever, and the customary mealtimes and corresponding restaurant hours are something completely different. The only thing that might possibly make matters worse is to be hungry, tired, and in search of food in England, Japan, or Scandinavia.

ENGLAND

Although hot, spicy, garlic-rich Indian cuisine is a favorite fare in England today, for the Brits, keeping away from garlic has been more than just a matter a tradition and taste—it was also an historical, social statement.

Garlic was considered to be a peasant-only food and the smell of garlic on the body or breath locked one firmly down in the lower class.

In fact, looking back into British history, any association with garlic was considered unsavory. As a sign of the times, William Shakespeare poked fun at the plebian, pungent people in his plays. In *Measure for Measure*, Act III, Scene II, Lucio disparages Duke Claudio and assigns garlic breath to the destitute by writing, "He's not past it yet, and I say to thee, he would mouth with a beggar, though she smelt brown bread and garlic: say that I said so. Farewell."

Let us say, "Farewell," "Cheers then!" or "Cheerio" to England—we're getting hungry!

JAPAN

Although garlic does show up in modern Japanese cuisine today, it is used sparingly. Traditional Japanese cooking uses just five basic flavors: miso, salt, soy, sugar, and vinegar. Garlic did not make the flavor list. Garlic was historically used for medicinal purposes only and did not find a place at the table until recently. The Japanese have always preferred, and still do prefer, that their food look and taste precisely like what it is—fresh, raw vegetables and fresh, raw fish with rice. Everything is simple, beautifully plated, and served with soy sauce.

SCANDINAVIA

The Scandinavians are not traditionally big garlic eaters and Scandinavian food tends to be fresh, either right out of the ocean or direct from the rich earth. This approach does not seem to be far from traditional Viking fare. Customary Scandinavian flavorings include cardamom, chives, dill, fennel, juniper berries, parsley, and thyme. No garlic. Dill has jokingly been referred to as the "garlic of the North" because the Scandinavians use it in just about anything. Although there are garlic-specific restaurants in many major Scandinavian cities today, most Scandinavians will still find many more uses for lingonberry jam than *Allium sativum.*

There is little doubt that England, Japan, and Scandinavia, the traditional garlic naysaying countries, bring at least a little something edible to the table. But let's be bold and get to garlic.

Let's Hear It for Garlic!

When the subject of garlic in international cuisine crops up, most Americans immediately think of Italy and mounds of great Italian pasta. Some say, "Szechuan!" (China) and others cry, "kimchi!" (Korea) or "curry!" (India). Many exclaim, "Middle Eastern!" But unless their ancestors were from abroad, it is hard to find an American who will reminisce over a garlic-heavy recipe that was handed down from Grandma. WASPish American grandmothers just never thought to use garlic, and neither did their mothers. Fortunately, we're a country of immigrants, so there was plenty of garlic to go around.

CHINA

GARLIC IN CHINESE: *hu suan* (garlic plant), *da suan* (garlic clove)

Not only are the Chinese the world's biggest producers of garlic, they are also the world's biggest consumers of it as well. The Chinese use garlic as glue, as a food preservative, and for plain old, everyday eating. The Chinese eat a *lot* of garlic and some even claim that they stay young and healthy by eating as many as eight to twelve cloves a day.

The use of garlic in China goes back to 600 B.C.E. and is heralded in the *Shih Ching*, a collection of traditional Chinese odes and ballads that describes everyday life in the highlands of Shensi. Much later on the garlic timeline, Marco Polo, during his travels in the thirteenth century, marveled at watching strong, healthy Chinese eat finely chopped raw meat with raw minced garlic. Today, people of all ages, from all around the world, seek out these very same ingredients when frequenting Chinese restaurants, albeit thoroughly cooked.

If you take the time to watch the garlic cult movie *Garlic Is as Good as Ten Mothers*, you can see Henry of Henry's Hunan Restaurant in San Francisco (*www.henryshunanrestaurant.com*) demonstrating his sizzling wok at work—if only movies could smell!

My standout favorite Chinese dishes with garlic are eggplant in garlic sauce and Szechuan beef.

FRANCE
GARLIC IN FRENCH: *Ail*

Four Thieves Vinegar protected the opportunistic French scoundrels who robbed dead plague victims in the late 1700s. But the best and most civilized way to enjoy garlic in France is to simply eat it.

In France, garlic is primarily the providence of the Provençe region, located in the southeastern region of France. Provençe is the part of France that touches the Mediterranean Sea, and snuggles up against Italy. Provençe brings all things wonderful to mind—endless lavender fields, rosemary-lined walkways, mammoth markets filled with artichokes and sausages and the freshest herbs, fruits, and vegetables imaginable.

Yes, France just might have the best of everything edible, including pistou, a garlic, tomato, and cheese mix that is added to soup, and aioli, the traditional garlic and olive oil mayonnaise that goes with just about everything from meat to frites. Aioli is a composite of two French words for garlic and oil: ail and huile. *Plus d'aioli, s'il vous plait,* or in English, more aioli, please.

My standout favorite French dishes with garlic are aioli and chicken with forty cloves of garlic.

GERMANY
GARLIC IN GERMAN: *Der Knoblauch*

Although Germany is not particularly well known for using garlic in traditional, German cuisine, the Germans have been pioneers and scientific leaders when it comes to studying the effectiveness of garlic as a means of preventing or reducing the risk of heart disease. Germany's "Commission E" governmental agency evaluated hundreds of herbal remedies and when it came to garlic, their official findings were:

▸ One medium clove of fresh garlic daily is a preventative measure for artery health.
▸ Garlic is helpful in individuals with elevated blood lipids.
▸ Garlic has antibacterial and antifungal qualities.
▸ Garlic inhibits platelet aggregation.
▸ Garlic lowers blood lipids.
▸ Garlic prolongs bleeding and blood-clotting time.
▸ Garlic helps dissolve blood clots and helps heal wounds.

GREECE

Garlic in Greek: *Skordon*

The Greeks are responsible for many great things—the first cookbook ever (by Archestratus in 320 B.C.E.), the gods, and the Great Games (The Olympics), for example.

**Give me a word, any word, and I show you
that the root of that word is Greek.**

—NICK PORTOKALOS IN THE MOVIE *MY BIG FAT GREEK WEDDING*

What garlic the ancient Greeks did not feed to the athletes to improve performance prior to the Great Games, they sent off with the cooks to the kitchen and out came roasted lamb—with garlic, of course. The Greeks also used garlic oil for personal protection as they gathered the roots and leaves of the poisonous hellebore plant to use in warfare. And they ate garlic.

GARLIC QUIZ: Which of the following Greek delicacies traditionally contain no garlic?

1. Dolmades
2. Tzatziki
3. Baklava
4. Spanakopita
5. Kourabiethes
6. Tsoureki

Answer: 1, 3, 4, 5, and 6 traditionally contain no garlic.

*Delicious Bites:
Greek Delicacies*

- *Dolmades* are tender grape leaves stuffed with meat or rice.
- *Tzatziki* is a cold yogurt-based sauce with cucumbers, garlic, olive oil, and dill for drizzling over grilled meat.
- *Baklava* is a sweet, sticky, honey-and-walnut dessert made with phyllo dough pastry.
- *Spanakopita* is a spinach-and-cheese pie made with phyllo dough pastry.
- *Kourabiethes* are shortbread-like butter Christmas cookie balls with toasted almonds that are covered in powdered confectioner's sugar.
- *Tsoureki* is a traditional, sweet Easter bread that is often baked with colorful hardboiled Easter eggs pressed right into the dough.
- My standout favorite Greek dishes with garlic are lamb roast, gyros with fresh tomatoes, slices of onion, and tzatziki on hot, thick, squishy, white pita bread.

Of the many smells of Athens two seem to me
the most characteristic—that of garlic, bold
and deadly like acetylene gas, and that of dust,
soft and warm and caressing like tweed.

—EVELYN WAUGH, AUTHOR

INDIA

Garlic in Hindi: *Lashun*

Garlic has an esteemed place in traditional folk medicine as well as on the dining table in India. The ancient, Indian Ayurvedic medicine system identified garlic as a fire and water or "Pitta" food and prescribed garlic to boost both passion and energy. Garlic was so pungent and such as passion booster, however, that some Indian religions prohibited their spiritual leaders from eating it.

The basic three Gs of Indian cuisine are garlic, ginger, and green chilies, which just might explain why curry dishes are often served with a pitcher of water—or two.

My standout favorite Indian dishes with garlic are any kind of curry and garlic naan.

ITALY

GARLIC IN ITALIAN: *Aglio*

Most people are surprised to learn that traditional, Italian cuisine is quite basic and does not always include garlic. In fact, the book *Garlic and Oil: Food and Politics in Italy* concludes that Italian cuisine is a "cuisine of scarcity." This is shocking because it is quite contrary to the reputation that Italian food has garnished.

Throughout history, the majority of Italians spent their lives in relative poverty and under someone's rule. Under Mussolini's fascist reign (1923–1939), austerity was a prescribed way of life in Italy. Italians were asked to rely on the basic foods that they could produce themselves in a countrywide effort to be self-sufficient, a national political policy known as "autarky." There was very little to eat after World War II, and what food people did have was grown on the family farm.

Today, traditional Italian food is still a basic, easy-to-prepare fare. Perhaps it is so delicious because of its simplicity—and the fact that it's easy to eat so darn much of it. So put that bathroom scale away for a few days and just say *"buon appetito!"*

Stomach-Filling Food

The only bad thing about Italian food is that you're hungry again in three days.

So just eat again.

My standout favorite Italian dishes with garlic are spaghetti a aglio, linguine with clam sauce, spaghetti carbonara, and pasta pesto.

KOREA

GARLIC IN KOREAN: *Mah-nuhl*

For anyone who is not Korean, kimchi is most certainly an acquired taste. Kimchi is a very spicy side dish that is made from cabbage and daikon radish. The inherently bland cabbage and daikon are revved up by fermenting them in a brine made from garlic, ginger, scallion, fish sauce, and chili paste. It's a super spicy concoction that is a traditional Korean staple and health food. It is usually placed on the table at every meal as a side dish and is said to lower cholesterol, to keep arteries clear, and to promote digestion. This sounds exactly like a prescription monograph for *Allium sativum*.

My standout favorite Korean dish with garlic is short ribs.

Tiger Deterrent

Koreans protected themselves against wild tiger attacks by eating large amounts of pickled garlic before they traveled along remote mountain paths. They believed that the pungent "eau de garlic" smell that exuded from their pores as they hiked would keep tigers away—tigers don't like garlic in their food.

MIDDLE EASTERN

GARLIC IN ARABIC: *Thoum*

There's no getting away from garlic in the Middle East. But then who would want to leave hummus, baba ganoush, or a great falafel behind in the dust, anyway?

Middle Eastern cuisine, that is the food from Egypt, Iran, Iraq, Israel, Lebanon, Saudi Arabia, Syria, and Turkey, incorporates garlic—and lots of it.

My standout favorite Middle Eastern dishes with garlic are hummus and baba ganoush.

SPAIN

GARLIC IN SPANISH: *Ajo*

The majority of the garlic sold throughout Europe today is grown in Spain. The Spanish are famous for using garlic in cold gazpacho soup, to cure sausages and meats such as chorizo, and to spice up the ultimate, one-dish meal paella, prepared and served in a giant, cast-iron paella pan.

The availability of food in the post-World War II years in Spain was not too different from Italy—the food that was available was grown on family farms and there was not a lot of it. Bread topped with sliced tomatoes, sliced garlic, olive oil, and sprinkled salt made many a meal.

My standout favorite Spanish tapas dishes with garlic are patatas bravas and pan amb tomate.

UNITED STATES

Garlic in English: *Garlic*

Garlic does not factor into traditional North American cuisine, but because the major U.S. cities were comprised of pockets of distinct, ethnic neighborhoods, garlic was introduced to Americans by osmosis. But just because it couldn't be avoided on the city streets did not mean it found easy entry into the American pantry.

Garlic was first grown commercially in California in the 1920s. But it was not until the late 1970s and early 1980s that garlic became truly popular in the States.

Jokingly referred to as "the drug of the eighties," garlic's strong smell and the fact that the older generation didn't use or like it made garlic controversial and therefore even more appealing. Garlic came after "Sex, Drugs, and Rock and Roll" at a time when young adults needed to unite behind a new cause. Garlic brought people together again and became a symbol of independence and rebellion.

Lloyd John Harris deserves most of the credit for starting the American garlic revolution in the late 1970s and early 1980s. His efforts quickly raised garlic eating to cult status all across America. From his Berkeley, California vantage point, Harris founded the garlic fan club, Lovers of the Stinking Rose, and wrote his two great-to-this-very-day garlic books *The Book of Garlic* and *The Official Garlic Lovers Handbook*.

Although it would have been wonderful to have the page space and the time to test and include all of the recipes for our favorite dishes mentioned here, it just wasn't possible. However, the following essential, life-changing recipe can't be omitted and I would be remiss as an author and garlic lover if I did not include this one. This healthy garlic salad dressing is so easy it's ridiculous, and you'll come out smelling like a hero of the stinking rose.

Healthy Garlic Salad Dressing

ABOUT THIS RECIPE

My friend Brigitte Fox is a registered dietician. She is also a health nut, not because she wants to be, but because she *has* to be. Brigitte has food allergies and spent many years and many thousands of dollars discovering the simple truth that is now the key to her wellness. Simply stated, eat foods as close to their natural form as possible and make sure that you can identify everything you put in your mouth. This recipe is a derivation of Brigitte's salad dressing and it has become a garlicky favorite for literally all of my friends. Everyone who eats it inevitably asks, "What's in this?" and then they are amazed by its simplicity. This recipe has made its way from California to Michigan, from New York to Seattle, and it has headed on down to Florida, too. Please try it, make it your own, and pass it along so that your friends can love it, too.

INGREDIENTS

Some canola oil

A few cloves of fresh garlic

Lots of salt

Lots of ground black pepper

A few thinly sliced fresh tomatoes

A few thinly sliced fresh red, yellow, or orange peppers

A handful or two of raisins, dried cherries, fresh grapes,
    or any fresh, sweet fruit (optional)

A handful or two of toasted or candied nuts

DIRECTIONS

1. Pour canola oil into the bottom of the wooden salad bowl. Crush the garlic cloves into the oil and add a generous amount of salt and pepper.
2. Mix thoroughly with a wooden spoon, holding the bowl at an angle to form a pool of oil and spices. Add the thinly sliced tomatoes and pepper rings.
3. Mix again, coating vegetables thoroughly with oil. Season with additional salt and pepper to taste. Add raisins, dried cherries, grapes, or diced fresh fruit and mix thoroughly again.
4. Add red leaf or butter lettuce immediately before serving so that the lettuce stays crisp. Toss it thoroughly, then add most of the nuts and toss again. Sprinkle with remaining nuts.
5. Make the dressing in a wooden salad bowl if you can. My wooden salad bowl has the distinct honor of being known as "the magic salad bowl" amongst the girlfriends, but I have also made it in a glass bowl and it still tastes great. Prepare the dressing an hour or so ahead of eating time and just let it sit in the bowl while you prepare the rest of the meal. This lets the juices from the tomatoes, peppers, and fruits flavor the oil. Serve with warm, fresh French bread.

Tomatoes and oregano make it Italian; wine and tarragon make it French. Sour cream makes it Russian; lemon and cinnamon make it Greek. Soy sauce makes it Chinese; garlic makes it good.

—ALICE MAY BROCK

CHAPTER 4

MYSTICAL, MAGICAL GARLIC: MYTHS AND LEGENDS

Vampires and potions and witches—oh my! Garlic's natural power to amaze and mystify humankind predates written history. Magical and mystical, mythological and legendary, garlic's reputation for repelling evil has endured even to this very day. Chances are good that anyone you ask about garlic today will mention one of the following myths or legends from long, long ago.

Satan Started It

It comes as no surprise to learn that Satan started it all as the insidious star of the leading garlic legend. Although it has proven impossible for us to locate a verifiable source, research indicates that once Satan spoiled everything for all of humankind, he fled the Garden of Eden and left two footprints. According to both Muslim and Christian legends, garlic sprouted in his left footprint, and onions grew in his right footprint. Were the garlic and onions residual evils left behind by Satan, like litter? Or was it the good earth giving him a great big, green flip-off as a gesture of retaliation and good riddance? You'll have to decide for yourself.

Egyptians—Garlic to Go

The Egyptians harnessed the earthly powers of garlic and used it as a currency, in medicine making, as a strength-boosting food for the pyramid builders, and even in the embalming process. But the Egyptians also believed that garlic was sacred and that it held magical powers to ward off evil in both life and death. They placed fresh garlic cloves and whole heads of garlic in tombs to ensure their rulers were well-supplied on the journey into the afterlife. Garlic—Egyptians did not leave life without it.

Greek Mythology and Magic

In Homer's epic poem *The Odyssey*, eating garlic protected Odysseus from goddess Circe's poison that was powerful enough to turn other non-garlic-eating men promptly into pigs. Mythology aside, Greek historian and author Theophrastus (372–288 B.C.E.) wrote of garlic being placed on stones at intersections to confuse and distract Hecate, the goddess of magic, witchcraft, and raising of the dead. The Greeks used garlic to protect themselves from poison potions and to bewilder witches.

The Middle Ages

In the Middle Ages, people of all classes believed that garlic was a super power. Garlic's medicinal might and its culinary capacity were common knowledge, passed down from generation to generation. Garlic was a readily available problem-solving powerhouse and everyone had witnessed garlic in action firsthand at home as part of daily life. Garlic cured ailments literally from head (earaches and toothaches) to toe (toenail fungus and snakebites), but no one had even the faintest idea what made garlic so powerful. If garlic was so almighty that it could prevent and cure disease right before the eyes, it was also likely capable of protecting people from the other primary, pending peril—the onslaught of evil.

In the Middle Ages, garlic was worn, stashed, slathered, eaten, drunk, grown, and hung as protection from both illness and evil. Garlic protected against evil creatures and against the evil eye—bad wishes and bad luck. Here are some ways our ancestors used garlic to ward off physical and paranormal problems:

▶ **Around the neck:** Herbalists recommended wearing garlic necklaces and eating a lot of garlic to avoid succumbing to sickness. Individual garlic cloves were strung on thread to form a necklace or garland and worn around the neck for purification and protection.

▶ **For the baby:** Cradles of newborns were adorned with garlic to protect the newcomers from being snatched by evil spirits. A good midwife always ensured that there was plenty of garlic in the house to protect both mother and child at birthing time.

▸ **In the belly:** Garlic was served daily at meals, even for breakfast. Garlic was soaked in wine and vinegar, and the resulting beverage was consumed as a plague deterrent throughout Europe.

▸ **On the body:** The garlic-and-vinegar beverage that provided people protection from illness was so powerful that it was used by a band of French thieves who busied themselves by pickpocketing thousands of dead people who had fallen victim to the plague. Slipping their hands into the pockets of dead people without being noticed was not the hard or hazardous part of the job for these opportunistic thieves. Avoiding the plague was the riskiest part of the business and they took every precaution. They not only drank the garlic-and-vinegar mixture, they doused themselves in it—and the rest is history.

Four Thieves Vinegar was officially born, brewed, bottled, and sold in Marseilles France in 1720. It can still be purchased today. If you're a BIYer (a brew it yourselfer), you'll find many recipes for Four Thieves Vinegar online. For instance, check out *www.theherbgardener* *.blogspot.com.*

▸ **In the garden:** Garlic was planted in everyday gardens for family consumption, but garlic also found a place along the borders of mystical "cosmic gardens" and the medicinal monastic gardens that cropped up during the Middle Ages.

Eastern Europe

Slovakian folklore favored using garlic to repel evil of all kinds. It was a legendary belief that evil spirits stayed away from bad smells and, as a result, garlic was placed in the mouths, ears, and nostrils of corpses as a means of warding off evil spirits. This practice was similar to the embalming methods used by the ancient Egyptians.

Vampires

No discussion of garlic would be complete without reference to vampires and their alleged aversion to it. When I found myself weak on vampire expertise, I read, I searched, and I asked around in preparation for this chapter. What I quickly discovered startled me. They are among us—well, the vampire lovers, at least. For years, I have been alongside of them every day. Not just one, not just two, but three vampire aficionados have been lunging and jumping right next to me in Jazzercise class. It's been happening for years and I never knew it. They are the types you'd never suspect, completely undercover—a grandmother, an accountant, and a retired schoolteacher. A summary of my multimedia discoveries, as they relate to garlic, follows.

Garlic versus Bloodsuckers

Blood-seeking, stealthy, vampire-like creatures exist as part of folk traditions in many cultures around the world. Garlic is the one thing that, across the board, renders their powers utterly useless.

Eastern Europe is the land of the vampire, which explains the vampire's accent and why so many vampire legends take place in countries like Romania (home of the historical and legendary Transylvania), Slovakia, and Serbia. In Eastern Europe, when the vampire security threat level was high, a vampire scout was sent out to roam the streets with garlic hidden in his pocket. Vampires he encountered would recoil, thereby identifying themselves.

"Good Eeeeevening!"

Count Dracula is the world's oldest and most famous vampire who demonstrated an aversion to garlic. Irish author Bram Stoker's novel *Dracula*, published in 1897, demonstrated garlic's use for protection against vampire attacks and also as a means of ensuring that dead vampires did not rise again. So long as the beautiful Lucy Westenra wore the garlic necklace that was made for her, she was safe from attack. When Lucy was not wearing her necklace, the opportunistic Count Dracula moved in and sucked her in and over to the vampire side. When Lucy was finally killed by means of stake through the heart, the fearless band of vampire hunters beheaded her and stuffed her mouth full of garlic to make sure she stayed dead.

Following the Rumanian tradition, garlic is used in excess to keep the vampires away . . . Following the Jewish tradition, a dispenser of schmaltz [liquid chicken fat] is kept on the table to give the vampires heartburn if they get through the garlic defense.

—CALVIN TRILLIN

Today, vampires still need to stay out of the sun and are active in the daytime only when it's dreary and overcast. Although they are most comfortable at night, in dark shadows, or in the twilight hours, today's vampires are attractive and mainstream—they might even seem almost ordinary to you. Until you touch them, that is, or get close enough to hear them not breathing. Modern vampires are forever young, cute, sensitive, professional, and popular. They have to move every few years so no one notices that they never age, but they manage to have successful jobs. They own bars, and their acute sense of taste and smell make them excellent restaurateurs. Some are even physicians who practice incredible self-restraint.

What's more, only old-fashioned, old-school vampires have an aversion to garlic. Times have changed and modern-day vampires think the whole garlic thing is a ridiculously silly joke. It makes them laugh.

It Doesn't Always Work

Just because garlic has worked in the past to keep away vampires doesn't mean it's always going to be that way. In the incredibly popular *Twilight* series, author Stephenie Meyer follows certain rules in writing about vampires: no fangs, no coffins, no stakes through the heart, and no garlic.

Keeping Romania Safe from Vampires

Joke or no joke, traditional "Guarding the Garlic" celebrations are still held in Romanian homes today on St. Andrew's Eve (the evening of November 29). It was believed that wolves and vampires came out in force to hunt on St. Andrew's Eve, so garlic is rubbed on doors and windows for ceremonial protection from evil. Even cows and other animals get a garlic rubdown. Garlic bulbs that represent the family's children are placed in bowls in groups of three and are guarded carefully overnight by family matriarchs. Romanians also bring out extra garlic to keep vampires and other evils away on St. George's Eve (the evening of April 22).

Whether it's true blood, the synthetic stuff (blood type S?) ordered up neat at Merlotte's Bar & Grille, or just a figure of speech, vampires have a long and dark history of blood-getting and sucking the life right out of you. And whether you believe in vampires or not, keep in mind that garlic does repel the bloodsuckers of the insect world: mosquitoes (see Chapter 5, *Insect Repellent and Pest Deterrent*).

Witches—For and Against Garlic

Throughout history, everyday mortals used garlic to protect themselves, their families, their livestock, and all of their earthly belongings against witches, sorcerers, and evil, meddlesome spells. Interestingly enough, the reverse is also true. Garlic was—and still is—carried by witches for protection against evil and is used as an ingredient in love potions and home protection spells. Such is the mystery of garlic.

Love potions and protection spells? Who couldn't use some of these? What superstitious people labeled "witchcraft" was most likely the practice of concocting herbal remedies and employing good old folk medicine (see Chapter 5, *Folk Medicine and Natural Cures*).

Garlic in the Ring

Traditional Spanish bullfighters were known to carry cloves of garlic into the ring for protection.

GARLIC FROM A TO Z

Here's everything you wanted to know about this miraculous vegetable. Sit back, enjoy a big bowl of garlic ice cream, and browse through this miscellany.

Architecture

Alliums, mainly the onion (*Allium cepa*), appear in architecture, largely in Eastern Europe. Travel to Russia, for example, and you'll see them everywhere—as onion domes. Perched up high on churches and cathedrals, often in clusters, onion domes are typically capped with crosses. They look like oversized, over-the-top onions, hence the name. You will find bunches of onion-domed churches in Austria, the Czech Republic, and Germany, as well as in India, the Middle East, and Central Asia.

Leave it to Spanish architect Antoni Gaudí (1852–1926), however, to garnish his work with, not onions, but garlic (*Allium sativum*). Travel to Barcelona, Spain and you'll see how Gaudí pushed the outside of the architectural envelope by putting garlic domes on Casa Batlló (*www.casabatllo.es*), a formerly ugly apartment building he was commissioned to restore in 1904. The restoration work was completed in 1906, and now this notorious, art nouveau building is the next stop for tour busses filled with Gaudí gawkers—right after his most famous project, La Sagrada Familia.

Art

It's no surprise that garlic, the illustrious *Allium sativum*, pops up in paintings from various periods. Spanish realism painter Diego Velazquez, for instance, painted *Kitchen Scene with Christ in the House of Martha and Mary* (1618), more commonly known as *A Young Woman Crushing Garlic*. This work is now preserved in London's National Gallery.

Later, Post-Impressionists Renoir and Van Gogh had a go at it. Both garlic and onions were focal points in *The Onions* (1881), an impressionist painting by Renoir. Van Gogh's *Still Life with Bloaters and Garlic* (1887) shows bloaters, sizeable sardine-like fish, alongside a big bulb of—you guessed it—garlic.

If you're a fine art poster collector who loves garlic and the Arts & Crafts style, you might want to purchase a signed copy of the poster entitled *Garlic Festival* by David Lance Goines. This collectible poster was created for the Chez Panisse Garlic Festival that was held July 12–16, 1977. (Chez Panisse is the name of famed chef Alice Waters's restaurant in Berkeley, California.) Have a look at *www.goines.net* or watch the movie *Garlic Is as Good as Ten Mothers* to see the original poster, which hangs at the Chez Panisse restaurant. Now *this* would make a great garlic gift for a favorite guy or gal!

Business

Garlic is big business on a global scale with imports and exports, international meetings, tariffs and duties designed specifically to protect local garlic growers.

Top Ten Global Garlic Producers

The top ten garlic-producing countries are, in order of production:

1. China
2. India
3. South Korea
4. Russia
5. The United States
6. Spain
7. Egypt
8. Turkey
9. Thailand
10. Brazil

The total area devoted to garlic production worldwide has more than doubled since 1970. Today, there are more than 2 million acres of farmland around the world producing about 10 million tons of garlic annually.

China, specifically China's Shandong province, supplies an estimated 75 percent of the world's garlic in spite of the fact that many countries around the world have instituted tariffs and taxes to protect domestic garlic growers.

U.S. Garlic Imports and Exports

The United States imported more than 430 million pounds of garlic in 2010, valued in excess of $178 million. Close to 165 of the 430 million pounds were fresh garlic, which accounted for $130 million. The remaining 265 million pounds were processed, dried garlic for use in food processing.

In 2010, the United States exported 43.1 million pounds of fresh and processed garlic combined. United States fresh garlic exports to Mexico and Canada alone were an estimated 18.6 million pounds, valued at $16.4 million in 2010.

U.S. Garlic Consumption

When it comes to eating members of the allium family, the United States alone consumes about 400 million pounds of fresh garlic each year, second only to onions, *Allium cepae.*

GARLIC QUIZ: What are the edible members of the allium family?

1. Leeks
2. Shallots
3. Horseradish
4. Chives
5. Ginger
6. Scallions
7. Garlic
8. Onions

ANSWER: 1, 2, 4, 6, 7, and 8 are all members of the allium family. Horseradish (*Armoracia rusticana*) is a member of the Brassicaceae family. Ginger (*Zingiber officinale*) is a member of the Zingiberaceae family.

California Leads U.S. Softneck Garlic Production

California produces more than eighty percent of the commercially grown softneck garlic (silverskin and artichoke varieties). In the United States sixty percent of the yield is dehydrated for use in processed and prepared foods for humans and to flavor pet food.

America's largest garlic producer is the family-owned and operated Christopher Ranch, located in Gilroy, California, about forty miles south of San Jose. Christopher Ranch was established in 1956 and devotes about 6,000 acres of rich farmland to garlic production.

Large-scale growers, like Christopher Ranch, focus on softneck garlic primarily because it does not produce a stiff seed stalk and is therefore the easiest variety to prepare (harvest, cure, and clean) and store. It is good garlic and the only kind that most people know from the grocery store, however, softneck garlic is not a particularly great tasting garlic. It is best suited for dehydration and use in processed food products, which is exactly why the large-scale producers grow it. By the time it gets to the grocery store, a pound of ordinary, softneck garlic costs about $4.

World Congress on Garlic

The first World Congress on Garlic was held in Washington, D.C., in 1990. It was the first, formal gathering of garlic researchers who presented results of their studies on the role garlic plays in lowering cholesterol and in fighting cancer and cardiovascular disease. The meeting stimulated additional garlic research within specific, focused medical communities. As a result, garlic study results are now frequently presented at industry-specific meetings focused on food, nutrition, cardiology, cancer, and hair, to name a few. The Garlic Congress 2011 that was to be held in Kyoto, Japan was cancelled due to the tsunami-spawned, 2011 Tōhoku earthquake and subsequent nuclear disaster.

Garlic Tariffs and Duties

In 2004, garlic imports from China surpassed U.S.-grown garlic for the first time and the U.S. government stepped in. But in spite of the 377 percent tariff the U.S. government imposed on garlic imports to protect domestic growers, China still controls the world's garlic production, driving more than half of the U.S. large-scale garlic growers right out of the garlic business. Along similar lines, the European Union has levied a 9.6 percent *ad valorem* duty on all garlic imports plus a 1,200 euros per ton additional levy for shipments over a specified quota.

Smaller, Specialty Growers Grow Greater Garlic

Hardneck garlic is where the flavor is. It may not store as long as softneck garlic and is not supple enough to be easily braided, but hardneck garlic is more pleasing to the palate and has greater health benefits.

If you're the hard-working, entrepreneurial sort, gourmet garlic may be just the new frontier you've been looking for. In the United States, many smaller, specialty garlic growers are busy producing the hardneck "gourmet" garlics—and they're making a go of it. "Buy local" trends and the increasing popularity of local farmers' markets have made it possible for smaller farmers to prosper with delicious specialty crops such as hardneck garlic, leaving the boring bulbs to the big players. Keep in mind, though, that garlic growing is not the kind of business that lends itself easily to automation—garlic is usually handled six or more times from planting to pantry. Growing garlic is decidedly low-tech. Although it's unlikely that you'll find hardneck garlic at the grocery store, your local farmers' market will have it once it has been harvested and cured. You can also purchase it online at anywhere from $12–$24 per pound. Look in the *Resources* section at the end of this book for growers.

Without garlic I simply would not care to live.

—LOUIS DIAT

Choose Fresh Garlic

If you're looking for great garlic, it is best to buy it at your local farmers' market where you can probably meet the guy or gal who grew it for you. They'll know where your garlic has been and how it's been treated all along the way.

If you are not able to find anything other than the typical grocery store garlic, go online and buy direct from an independent garlic grower. Gourmet Garlic Gardens offers an online cooperative farmers' market at *www.gourmetgarlicgardens.com* and you'll find more "buy direct" resources listed in the back of this book.

It's ideal to know the kind of garlic you're getting and where it comes from. Ask and learn something. We've been surprised to discover what produce purveyors know—and don't know—about the garlic they are selling.

It's best to buy only what you'll need to use for a few weeks. Fresh garlic, however, is seasonal and it is not always available. Garlic is harvested and cured in the summer months and it is at its freshest and best in summer and fall. If you find a variety of garlic that you love so much you can't bear the thought of ever being without it, ensure you have a cool, dry, dark, well-ventilated space at home and buy it up.

Various types and subspecies of garlic look, taste, and handle differently in the kitchen. But no matter the type, the criteria used to successfully select the best bulb in the bin remain the same.

If it's fresh, you'll find it loose so you can examine and choose your own. Fresh garlic will never be in a neat little cellophane package or bound tightly in a little mesh bag.

A good head of garlic is firm and hard with no green shoots and no soft spots—and it should not smell of garlic. Here are some specifics:

- Dry and clean—not dirty or moist (unless it's fresh out of the garden)
- Odorless—if garlic smells like garlic before it's crushed, it's rotting
- Plump and full—not shriveled up, no dents
- Skin wrappers intact—wrappers are papery and dry with no exposed cloves and no green shoots jutting out
- Stems stiff and hard—stems are more prominent in hardneck garlic varieties than in the softneck varieties

Old garlic bulbs smell like garlic, the wrappers are often moldy, and the outer cloves are often yellow and starting to shrivel. This is the beginning of what is formally called "waxy breakdown."

Old bulbs might even have green shoots popping out from cloves that are raring and ready to grow. Plant the cloves if you wish, and then throw that old garlic bulb away or toss it into your garden to help keep the pests away.

Cooking with Garlic

Garlic is a prolific vegetable with a long and spicy tradition, so it's no surprise that there are literally hundreds of cookbooks devoted exclusively to garlic cookery.

If you want to enjoy garlic's maximum health benefits, wait at least ten seconds after you cut or crush a clove of garlic before cooking it. This allows garlic's amino acid alliin to mix with its enzyme alliinase to produce allicin, garlic's healthful, healing powerhouse. Take your time when cooking garlic because cooking it too fast over high heat will cause it to burn and taste horribly bitter. Don't rush—always sauté garlic over medium-low heat. When it is the color of straw, remove it from the heat immediately—don't let it cook a second longer—or quickly add your other ingredients.

Garlic used as it should be used is the soul, the divine essence, of cookery. The cook who can employ it successfully will be found to possess the delicacy of perception, the accuracy of judgment, and the dexterity of hand which go to the formation of a great artist.

—MRS. W. G. WATERS, *THE COOK'S DECAMERON* (1901)

Blanching

Some people say that garlic cloves are easier to peel if they are blanched first. Others claim that blanching does not help at all and causes the garlic cloves to lose their flavor. So if you try blanching, be quick about it and toss the individual cloves into boiling water only very briefly (see *Peeling*).

Blending Garlic

Garlic is sticky when it is minced, crushed, or chopped—great news if you're using it for glue. But if it's destined for the dinner table, the stickiness can get in the way of a thorough garlic mix-in. Chop, mince, or crush the garlic as you normally would, and then combine it with another ingredient such as parmesan cheese or bread crumbs and mix those two ingredients together. The garlic will stick to the mix so it can be more consistently blended with the rest of the ingredients.

Sautéing

Sautéing brings out the best flavor of garlic. Always sauté garlic over low-to-medium heat—never use high heat. If the garlic sticks and is hard to move around in the pan, the heat is too high. Even if the garlic does not look burned, if it is cooked over high heat it may still taste bitter enough to ruin things. When in doubt, taste it—and don't be too proud to throw it out and start anew. With the exception of garlic bagels toasted with cream cheese, garlic that is browned is basically bad.

Blue Garlic

The acid in vinegar can sometimes cause marinated garlic cloves to turn bright blue. These colorful cloves are, however, still edible.

Chop or Crush?

The rougher you are with garlic as you prepare it, the stronger it tastes. It's a general rule of thumb that the smaller the piece of garlic, the more intense the flavor.

Clove Size?

Garlic clove sizes vary dramatically based on the variety of garlic. So, when a recipe calls for one clove of garlic, what does that mean? The rule of thumb is that 1 large garlic clove = 1 teaspoon of minced garlic.

Size Doesn't Matter

For me, the size of bulbs and the size of the cloves have no relationship to taste. Most people dislike small cloves because they are harder to peel. I grow varieties of garlic that are repeatedly small but they are repeatedly my favorites—every year. I no longer peel them when I use them in food. I just place them in one of those old-fashioned hand-held garlic presses (tip up, base down) and I press. I get almost 100 percent of the meat from the clove and just throw the skins away.

—CHESTER AARON, *WWW.CHESTERAARON.COM*

Roasting

Roasting brings out garlic's wonderfully rich, creamy, sweet, subtle, and nutty side. Roasting softens the flesh of the cloves so it is as easy to spread as butter, and a whole lot healthier. Whole heads of roasted garlic are easy to make and were a favorite among the ancient Greeks. You can bake them in the oven and even prepare them outside on the barbeque grill. Everyone will be surprised at the mellow taste. Among the many methods of roasting garlic, here are two that we like:

Oven-Roasted Garlic

▸ Use a sharp knife to cut the top off of the head of the garlic to expose the clove tops—about half an inch.
▸ Carefully remove the loose papery wrapper from the sides of the head, leaving some wrappers on to hold the cloves in place.
▸ Place the head of garlic in a small, ovenproof, glass baking dish or in a small, aluminum pan.
▸ Drizzle with 1 tablespoon of olive oil and 1 teaspoon of water.
▸ Sprinkle with salt and pepper.
▸ Wrap tightly with aluminum foil.
▸ Bake in a preheated 325-degree oven for 1 hour and 15 minutes.
▸ Remove from the oven, uncover, and baste with the pan juices.
▸ Return to oven and bake uncovered for 15 more minutes.

Roasted Garlic on the Grill

▸ Use a sharp knife to cut the top off of the head of the garlic to expose the clove tops—about half an inch.
▸ Carefully remove the loose papery wrapper from the sides of the head, leaving some wrappers on to hold the cloves in place.

▸ Place the garlic head on either two big pieces of heavy-duty aluminum foil or on four big layers of regular aluminum foil.

▸ Drizzle with 1 tablespoon of olive oil and sprinkle with salt and pepper.

▸ Wrap the bulb up like a Hershey's Kiss.

▸ Place it on the grill over medium-low, indirect heat with the grill lid on. If you are cooking on an open flame with no grill lid to keep the heat in, you will need to turn the garlic so it will cook evenly. In this case, be sure that the garlic is securely wrapped so the juices do not drain out when you turn it.

▸ Roast the wrapped garlic for 30 minutes to an hour. The garlic is done when it is soft.

▸ Unwrap, let cool, and enjoy warm or at room temperature. Squeeze the garlic cloves out of their wrappers directly onto bread, mash them with potatoes, spread them on pizza, put them in pasta, or eat them whole as is.

Safety When Handling Garlic

Once garlic cloves have been peeled or chopped, they should be used right away for best flavor as well as for safety. Garlic that is stored in oil presents a risk of food botulism.

Corn on the Cob

Ted Jordan Meredith, in his all-inclusive book *The Complete Book of Garlic: A Guide for Gardeners, Growers, and Serious Cooks,* suggests that you crush a few cloves of garlic (the hardneck rocambole variety is recommended), add salt, mash, add olive oil, mix, and drizzle over fresh corn. Ambrosia!

Equivalents

Nothing beats fresh garlic, but in a pinch, here are equivalents for garlic in minced, powder, juice, and salt forms. Be careful if you are substituting garlic salt for fresh garlic—be sure to reduce the amount of salt in the recipe overall. (See *Garlic Salt.*)

- 1 finely chopped medium clove = 1 teaspoon
- 3 finely chopped medium cloves = 1 tablespoon
- 12 finely chopped medium cloves = ¼ cup
- 1 small garlic clove = ½ teaspoon minced garlic
- 1 small garlic clove = ⅛ teaspoon garlic powder
- 1 small garlic clove = ¼ teaspoon garlic juice
- 1 small garlic clove = ½ teaspoon garlic salt

- 1 medium garlic clove = 1 teaspoon minced garlic
- 1 medium garlic clove = ¼ teaspoon garlic powder
- 1 medium garlic clove = ½ teaspoon garlic juice
- 1 medium garlic clove = 1 teaspoon garlic salt
- 1 large garlic clove = 2 teaspoons minced garlic
- 1 large garlic clove = ½ teaspoon garlic powder
- 1 large garlic clove = 1 teaspoon garlic juice
- 1 large garlic clove = 1 teaspoon garlic salt (same as 1 medium clove in order to reduce risk of over-salting)

Ethnic Alliums

- Garlic and scallions are the allium staples of cooking in northern China.
- Garlic and shallots are the allium staples of Thai cooking.

Garlic Salt

Garlic salt is a very high-sodium condiment that consists of salt, moisture-absorbing agents, and only a very tiny bit of garlic powder. The ratio is, at a minimum, about six to eight parts salt to one part garlic, so be sure to adjust your recipes accordingly if you are substituting with garlic salt.

Hints of Garlic

Garlic is at its mildest when it is roasted and at its most intense when it is raw and grated or pressed through a garlic press. To add garlic flavor to your sauce, soup, salad, or stew you can add roasted garlic or follow one of these suggestions that allows you to add garlic flavor without actually serving garlic to your guests.

For a hint of garlic in a soup, sauce, or stew, push a toothpick or skewer through peeled, whole cloves of garlic and add them to the pot while cooking. The toothpick makes the cloves easy to find and remove before serving. Be sure to pull out the same number of cloves that you put in.

For a hint of garlic in your salad, try one of these tips:

▶ Rub a wooden salad bowl with a freshly cut clove of garlic before making and tossing the salad in the bowl. (Note: Some people claim that over time this will ruin a wooden bowl because the residual garlic oils that seep into the wood will eventually turn rancid.)

▶ Make and use a chapon. A chapon is a dry crust of bread that is rubbed all over with a freshly cut clove of garlic. Drop the chapon into the salad bowl filled with greens, add the dressing, toss the salad, remove and discard the chapon, and serve the salad immediately.

Peeling

Peeling garlic is usually easy unless the clove is very fresh. To peel a clove of garlic, lay the clove on a clean work surface and then press down on it with the heel of your hand. The clove will flatten, pop open, and the skin loosens. If the skin does not fall right off, it can be pulled away easily with your fingers. If this doesn't work, get out your chef's knife and see *Smashing* under *Prep Methods* or see *Blanching* if you have a lot of cloves to peel.

The following alternative peeling method comes from Cafe Beaujolais in Mendocino, California. It produces not only peeled cloves of garlic, but also garlic oil for use in salad dressings and sautés. In her book *Cafe Beaujolais*, one-time owner-chef Margaret Fox shares this once-secret and now great kitchen tip of all time to ensure her immortality.

- Separate the garlic cloves from the bulb.
- Heat one cup of olive oil in a large frying pan to 230 degrees.
- Turn off the heat and add the garlic cloves.
- Stir the cloves gently to thoroughly coat with oil.
- After about fifteen seconds the cloves will be easy to peel. Don't leave them in much longer than that—they need to be in the oil for only a very short time.
- Remove the garlic cloves and slip off the peels.
- Use the remaining garlic oil for cooking.

Margaret Fox suggests storing the peeled cloves in the garlic oil once it has cooled and storing them in a covered container. (See *Safety*.)

Prep Methods

The way that garlic is prepared has a huge effect on the flavor. It's best to prep garlic by hand. Using a food processor or herb grinder tends to produce uneven pieces with different taste characteristics that don't blend well.

Once garlic has been prepped, use it right away. However, if you are prepping a lot of garlic and want to ensure that it doesn't discolor, place it in a small bowl and sprinkle a little salt on top. The salt helps to keep garlic from oxidizing and turning dark. Salt also prevents the garlic from sticking.

▸ **Grating**—grating garlic produces the finest mash with the most intense garlic flavor of all prep methods. Take a peeled clove of garlic and rub it carefully across a zester or a cheese grater.

▸ **Mincing**—minced garlic releases only a modest amount of garlic oil and produces a subtle, garlic flavor. You can watch a number of garlic-mincing demonstration videos online, but here are the basics. Place a peeled clove of garlic on a cutting board, trim off and discard the root end, cut the clove into thin strips lengthwise, turn the sliced clove (or the cutting board) 90 degrees, and slice across the strips to create small squares. Use a large chef's knife and a rocking motion to chop the small squares into even smaller pieces.

▸ **Pressing**—pressing garlic through a garlic press creates a smooth, garlic mash and releases a lot of flavorful oils. Pressed garlic has a strong garlic flavor and is the best method to use when the garlic is to be thoroughly mixed in. Pressing a garlic clove with the clove skin on decreases the amount of oil extruded and makes the garlic press easy to clean.

▸ **Smashing**—smashed garlic can be sautéed to impart its flavor and then discarded. Smash the clove by placing the broad, flat side of a kitchen knife (sharp edge pointing away from you) on the clove and then press down on the knife with the heel of your hand. This will smash the clove and pop the skin right off.

Press in a Pinch

Although no fully capable kitchen lacks a garlic press, you may occasionally find yourself without one or confronted with an unimpressive press to use. If this happens, don't be crushed—you are not foiled! Simply place the peeled cloves of garlic in a small dish and smash the cloves with the back of a spoon. Add a small amount of salt and smash again—the salt granules help to break the garlic down even further to a creamy, mashed-potato-like consistency.

Cult Film

Garlic Is as Good as Ten Mothers, directed by Les Blank, is a documentary film from 1980 that has achieved cult status. A visual blast from the past, it is filled with fiddling, feasts, and enormous quantities of garlic—we love it!

Filmed on location at the Gilroy Garlic Festival (*www.gilroygarlicfestival .com*), in the garlic fields somewhere between Gilroy and Salinas, at Flint's BBQ in Oakland, California (now closed but not forgotten), at Henry's Hunan Restaurant in San Francisco (*www.henryshunanrestaurant.com*), and in Berkeley, California at Alice Waters's infamous Chez Panisse restaurant (*www.chezpanisse.com*), *Garlic Is as Good as Ten Mothers* documents the "garlic revolution." It covers the history, lore, cultivation, and culinary use of garlic. In a series of interviews, international chefs, farmers, regular cooks, authors, and historians pour their hearts out as they prepare monumental feasts, talk about their relationship with garlic, and essentially declare their love of the "stinking rose."

The film features interviews with Lloyd John Harris, founder of the first and only garlic fan club, "Lovers of the Stinking Rose," and author of *The Book of Garlic* and *The Official Garlic Lovers Handbook*. Harris's 1980s vision of future forms of prepared garlic and his wish to bring small, independent garlic growers together for better business and greater garlic distribution demonstrates that he was a true visionary.

In 2004, *Garlic Is as Good as Ten Mothers* was given the great honor of being selected by the U.S. Library of Congress for preservation in the U.S. National Film Registry, which as of 2010 consisted of only 550 titles.

I found this essential garlic-lovers' movie quite hard to locate, but I was finally able to purchase a copy in DVD format online from The Garlic Store. Visit The Garlic Store at *www.thegarlicstore.com* for this movie and many more garlic-focused essentials . . . including garlic.

Decorating with Garlic

Decorating with food is an easy and earthly pleasure. Today, decorating with food can be as simple as showing off your fresh potatoes, onions, or tomatoes in a big bowl on the kitchen counter or table. But decorating with garlic once had a more practical purpose. During the Middle Ages, people hung garlic on doors and windows to repel evil spirits and to deter disease. These days, garlic braids, holiday wreaths, and garlands are carefully assembled by hand annually after the fall garlic harvest. At home, you can hang them as a convenient curing and storage method and as edible, attractive accoutrements for the home and kitchen. Be sure not only to stop and smell the garlic hanging in your kitchen but to use it as well because although it makes for delightful décor it won't last for more than a season.

In general, under the best of conditions garlic bulbs only last three to six months. Garlic keeps best in a cool, well-ventilated, dark, dry environment and does not last long in direct sunlight. Keep this in mind when you hang your garlic decorations.

Fresh, whole garlic bulbs do not have an odor, so if you smell garlic when you walk by your garlic braid or wreath, the garlic is starting to decay. When this happens, it's time to disassemble it and inspect each bulb carefully to determine which ones are harboring rotting cloves or are growing. Discard the rotting cloves, plant the cloves with green shoots, and get cooking with the rest.

DIYers will find more easy ways to decorate with garlic. Ellen Spector Platt offers some creative decorating and curious craft ideas that cleverly combine the textures and shapes of both onions and garlic in her book entitled *Garlic, Onion, & Other Alliums.*

Elephant Garlic

When an elephant is in the room, you have a few choices. You can hope that it simply goes away. You can choose to mention it—or not. In the case of garlic, however, we can't ignore the elephant—nor should we. And a quick look in the produce section of your local grocery store will tell you that the elephant is not going away any time soon. It has become very popular these days and is here to stay.

Surprise! We're talking about elephant garlic. In spite of its name, elephant garlic is not a true garlic (*Allium sativum*) at all. Rather, it is a misnamed member of the leek family—*Allium ampeloprasum*. What's more, elephant garlic, though hugely impressive in size, tastes like a leek and is therefore relatively mild. If you are looking for big, earthy, garlic taste, leave the elephant garlic behind and pick a real gourmet garlic . . . possibly a Polish White.

Is This the Garlic You're Looking For?

Can't find the garlic you want? Gourmet Garlic Gardens lets you buy direct from garlic growers across the United States without leaving your home. Visit Gourmet Garlic Gardens's online farmers' market at *www.gourmetgarlicgardens.com*—let your fingers do the shopping, eliminate the middlemen, and get the finest garlic you ever dreamed of delivered direct to your doorstop.

Entertainment

In 2008, Don Christopher, founder and president of Gilroy's garlic-producing giant, Christopher Ranch, and cofounder of the infamous Gilroy Garlic Festival, claimed he loves the business because "people have fun with garlic." Yes indeed, people have been having fun with garlic—and making fun of garlic—for ages. It's been going on for centuries.

Stop and smell the garlic! That's all you have to do.

—WILLIAM SHATNER

Theatrics

Greek playwright Aristophanes (446–388 B.C.E.) was probably the first to place garlic onstage in Athens in 424 B.C.E. Garlic first played a role in Aristophanes's fourth play, *The Knights*, a social and political satire that poked fun at everyday life in Athens during the Peloponnesian War (431–404 B.C.E.). In it, Demosthenes tells the sausage seller, "Well primed with garlic, you will have greater mettle for the fight," proof that Greeks recognized garlic as a powerful stimulant. Garlic was also mentioned as a wound healer, enemy deterrent, and cover-up technique for unfaithful wives in Aristophanes's subsequent plays.

William Shakespeare is no doubt the most famous and prolific playwright to include garlic in theatrical entertainment in 1595. In Act IV, Scene II of *A Midsummer Night's Dream* he suggested that actors without garlic breath would earn more favorable reviews from the critics.

And most dear actors, eat no onions nor garlic, for we are to utter sweet breath. And I do not doubt but to hear them say, "It is a sweet comedy."

—SHAKESPEARE

Festivals

Given the high regard in which garlic is held by cultures around the world, it should come as no surprise that there are many garlic festivals that bring people together to celebrate "the stinking rose" with food, contests, dances, vendors, parades, costumes, recipe books, and live music. You'll find many of them listed in the *Resources* section of this book.

California's first Gilroy Garlic Festival was held in 1979 in Gilroy, California, just forty miles south of San Jose. The festival was the brainchild of Don Christopher, whose family had been farming garlic around Gilroy since 1956.

Launched just two years after Alice Waters and Lloyd John Harris hosted a more intimate garlic festival at Chez Panisse Restaurant in Berkeley, California, the Gilroy Garlic Festival was the first large-scale garlic festival in the United States. It has since become the world's largest garlic festival and put Gilroy on the map. Don Christopher himself personally sees to it every year that the good garlic times go on there, ensuring the continued success of the festival he helped start more than thirty years ago. My how time flies when you're having fun—and eating a lot of garlic.

Folk Remedies and Natural Cures

A folk remedy is usually passed along by word of mouth as a cultural or family tradition. Folk medicines are made at home, not in a laboratory, and are often natural blends of herbs and other organic ingredients. Some folk remedies call for red wine or whiskey, no matter what the age of the patient.

Many such remedies are still in use today and continue to be passed down from generation to generation because they work. Most are easy to make from readily available ingredients and are cost-effective treatments. Some natural remedies offer even greater healing power than modern medicine, with fewer side effects. Natural remedies are in style again—it's all part of going green. They're linked to the practice of naturopathy, a philosophy of medicine that takes a holistic approach to healing.

It should come as no surprise that garlic has been a constant feature of natural medicine. Here are some of the ways that garlic has been used as a folk remedy and a natural cure:

Modern Medicine Concurs

When it comes to heart health, blood pressure, and cholesterol, modern medical studies have concluded that it's true: Garlic can help to prevent heart attacks and strokes by influencing the key variables that cause them—high cholesterol, high triglycerides, high blood pressure, and blocked arteries.

Aging

No matter what you do, the inevitable is going to happen, and in fact it is already happening to you at this very moment—you're getting older. Aging is cell damage, plain and simple.

Scientists believe that aging, and the devastating, heart-breaking diseases associated with aging—Alzheimer's disease, cancer, and heart disease, to name a few—are caused by "free oxidizing radicals," more commonly known simply as just "free radicals." Free radicals attack the DNA of a cell and disrupt normal cell growth. Anything you can do to eliminate free radicals will slow down the aging process as it manifests itself both inside and outside the body.

Although almighty garlic is not capable of stopping time, it is an antioxidant and eliminates free radicals, thereby helping you to maintain a sound mind and a healthy body. It might not be able to stop time, but garlic can help you keep up with time as it marches along. Garlic is also rich in selenium, a trace mineral known to fight cancer, particularly breast and prostate cancer. Garlic may also help to protect your vision as you age. The Macular Degeneration Association lists garlic as a key vision nutrient. Visit *www.maculardegenerationassociation.com* for more information and recommended doses.

There is no such thing as a little garlic.
—ARTHUR BAER, HUMORIST

Say "Yes!" to Garlic

It may make you feel old just hearing about all this, but keep in mind that you have quite a bit of control over what you eat and how you live your life—which translates into how healthy you are and how you feel. Some of the longest-living, most disease-free people on earth are that way because they live in low-stress societies and enjoy meals filled primarily with fresh fruits and vegetables and very little meat. No processed foods, no smoking, no drinking—no joke. It may sound like no fun, but the good part is that they are saying yes to garlic! The Chinese are great garlic eaters; in the Hunan province of China, some people eat more than fifty pounds of onions and garlic each year and claim it is the key to a long and healthy life.

Arthritis

Painful, stiff, swollen joints are a common complaint for many people over the age of fifty. The wear and tear of life erodes the protective cartilage between bones in the joints—and it hurts. Often the bones try to protect themselves and grow bone spurs that add to the agony. Many people turn to surgery to eliminate the problem, and even more turn to prescription, non-steroidal, anti-inflammatory drugs (NSAIDs) to ease the pain. Instead, consider a healthy, tasty alternative: garlic. The powerful sulfur compounds in garlic help to repair damaged cartilage and improve joint health.

Asthma

Garlic contains quercetin, a natural anti-inflammatory that helps to reduce airway inflammation in individuals with asthma, making it easier for them to breathe.

Atherosclerosis

When the linings of the arteries are caked with fatty cholesterol, a.k.a. plaque, circulation is impaired and the arteries become clogged, brittle, and stiff. In severe cases, arteries may become completely blocked, often leading to heart attack and stroke. Garlic reduces cholesterol and thins the blood— it offers a two-pronged approach to alleviating atherosclerosis.

Baldness

Heads up Rogaine! Garlic stimulates and nourishes the skin, kills off infection, and has been proven to get hair growing again. Garlic, applied topically and ingested, stimulates hair growth and has been successfully used as a remedy for baldness. It might just work for someone you know.

Bites and Stings

Garlic applied to the skin can prevent mosquito and other insect bites. It has also been used throughout history as a remedy for bee stings, dog bites, scorpion stings, and non-poisonous snakebites.

Snakebite Remedy

Protect the surrounding skin with petroleum jelly. Then make a garlic poultice by crushing or mincing a clove of garlic and placing it directly on the wound. Cover with gauze and tape it firmly in place. Leave the poultice on for no more than thirty minutes.

Cancer

Cancer cells are caused by carcinogens. Although carcinogens are everywhere—in the air, in food, and in the body—they are usually neutralized in the body and flushed out before they compound to form a tumor or wreak havoc with healthy tissues. Garlic reduces the development of carcinogenic or cancer-forming compounds in the body, thereby lowing the risk of many cancers, most notably esophageal, stomach, and bowel cancers. Bowel cancer has been shown to occur less frequently in people who eat a lot of raw garlic or take garlic supplements. Garlic's selenium, an antioxidant, is particularly helpful for patients with lung cancer.

Cold Sore

Garlic is an antibiotic, as well as a fungicide and a bactericide, and can help cure a cold sore. Smear a thin layer of Vaseline on the cold sore and place a thin slice of freshly cut garlic on top of the Vaseline. The Vaseline will hold the garlic slice in place. Keep the garlic slice on the cold sore for twenty to thirty minutes at a time. Repeat several times daily until the cold sore has healed.

Colds and Coughs

Individuals with robust immune systems are most likely to remain free of colds all year long. Another way to gain the edge over germs is to eat garlic—as much as possible and any way possible—because garlic fights germs. Garlic's allicin and allium are the powerhouses responsible for a germ-fighting job well done.

In Eastern Europe and in Asia, garlic, milk, and honey were traditionally combined and given to babies and children to treat colds and coughs.

Finally, there's that old standard, chicken soup. Chicken soup is a cross-cultural folk remedy that packs a double punch—it combines the selenium in garlic with the selenium in chicken to create a powerful concoction that cures.

Corns and Calluses

Ugly and sometimes painful corns and calluses can be cured with garlic. Rub raw garlic or a few drops of garlic oil on the corn or callus.

AUTHOR'S FIELD NOTE

My brother, Todd, is short on words and long on knowledge. He claims to have known for decades about garlic's ability to fight colds and claims that it really works. When he feels a cold coming on, he sucks on a raw clove of garlic. That nips his cold in the bud. So the next time you feel a cold coming on, suck on a fresh garlic clove as if it were a lozenge.

Diabetes

Approximately 26.9 percent of Americans over the age of sixty-five have diabetes, according to the National Institute of Diabetes and Digestive and Kidney Diseases. Diabetes is a major cause of heart attack and stroke.

People who have diabetes are living in bodies that cannot effectively regulate blood sugar (glucose) levels due to problems producing the essential hormone insulin. Insulin is produced by the pancreas, and its job is to push sugar from the bloodstream directly into the body's cells for energy. If insulin is not pushing the sugar out of the blood effectively, the sugar stays in the blood and can cause tissue damage and vision problems, as well as kidney and heart disease (see *Heart and Cardiovascular Disease.*) Raw garlic helps lower both cholesterol and triglyceride levels, which improves the body's ability to produce insulin.

Earache

Folk wisdom suggests that sticking a raw clove of garlic in the ear canal—or for smaller ears, part of a clove—stops earaches. Alternatively, obtain garlic oil capsules from a health food store and put a few drops of garlic oil in the ear canal.

Fungus

Garlic is a natural inhibitor of fungus, yeast, and mold. In this capacity, it helps to clear up ringworm, dermatitis, athlete's foot, jock itch, and dandruff. Garlic is often successful at eliminating these problems when antibiotics fail—not to mention the fact that it's natural and cheaper than drugs.

Hangover

I know this isn't, strictly speaking, a health issue, but the French garlic soup, *Ailée*, may the first and best garlic hangover remedy ever.

Heart and Cardiovascular Disease

Garlic has been helping to fight heart disease for thousands of years. Garlic's sulfurous compounds, vitamins B and C, selenium, and manganese team up to lower blood pressure when the bulb is consumed regularly. Garlic also prevents blood clots and is believed to simulate the blood's own, natural ability to break down clots if they do form.

Many specific types of cardiovascular problems exist, but heart disease by any name is a leading cause of death around the world. The essence of the matter is that people with cardiovascular diseases are not able to get the proper amount of blood *to* the heart or *from* the heart to feed the body and the brain. By thinning the blood, garlic can help counteract many of the causes of heart disease, which include poor diet, obesity, lack of exercise, genetics, hardening of the arteries (see *Atherosclerosis*), hypertension (see *High Blood Pressure, Hypertension*), high cholesterol (see *High Cholesterol*), smoking, diabetes (see *Diabetes*), and even poor oral hygiene and gum disease (see *Toothache*).

Hemorrhoids

Hemorrhoids are painful, swollen veins in the rectum. Garlic's natural antibiotic and anti-inflammatory powers do just what needs to be done—they kill bacteria and reduce the swelling.

Hemorrhoid Remedy

Slather a small, peeled clove of garlic with vegetable or vitamin E oil. Sleep with it in your rectum overnight, and then poop the clove out in the morning. Honest.

Herpes

Herpes is more common than many people will admit to, but according to the Centers for Disease Control (CDC), more than sixteen percent of the U.S. population is harboring genital herpes. Wait! The CDC has even worse news for those of us who are, or who know someone who is still sexually active. Individuals with genital herpes are between two and three times more likely to acquire HIV, the dreaded virus that causes AIDS, than herpes-free folks. Garlic fights viruses and infection.

Hiccups

According to ancient Indian Ayurvedic medicine, garlic and peacock feather ashes are key components for curing any of the five distinct types of hiccups. Ayurvedic medicine classifies hiccups based on one of five root causes—dietary, psychological, exertion, lung and stomach disease, and constipation. Independent of the type of hiccup, it can be cured by a diet of horse gram bean soup, garlic, old rice, patola gourd, tender radish, lemon, goat's milk, and several daily doses of peacock feather ashes with honey.

High Blood Pressure, Hypertension

According to the World Health Organization, high blood pressure is anything over 160/90. Genetics, stress, obesity, salt intake, high cholesterol, overuse of alcohol and caffeine, smoking, and atherosclerosis are common causes of hypertension. Garlic is a common remedy that has been used for cardiovascular health for thousands of years. By thinning the blood it improves circulation.

High Cholesterol

Garlic helps to combat high cholesterol. If you're a strict vegetarian, the cholesterol in your body has been produced from within by your own liver or comes from sugar, alcohol, or processed grains. Having some cholesterol is a good thing because the body uses it to make bile, which in turn helps to digest fat. But when there is too much of it, it attaches itself to the artery walls and inhibits the flow of blood out of your heart and into the rest of your body. When garlic is crushed, it produces allicin, which contains sulfur. When the sulfur reacts with oxygen, powerful compounds such as diallyl disulfide are produced, providing the power to fight cholesterol.

Impotence

Now this is a big one. Impotence, more precisely called "erectile dysfunction" these days, is something to smirk at unless, of course, it's happening to you. Whether the cause is related to stress, high blood pressure, medication, diabetes, old age, alcohol, or something entirely different, it's just no fun and can keep a very good man down.

The thirteenth-century Hebrew treatise, the Sefer Hasidim, recommends eating warm, roasted garlic as a remedy against impotence. Garlic has played a prominent role in the food of the Jews throughout history and is openly acknowledged as an aphrodisiac. The Talmud states that garlic should be eaten on Fridays, the night for lovemaking. Garlic might just spice things up, because it stimulates blood flow.

Impotence Remedy

Fresh garlic crushed with freshly ground coriander and mixed with red wine.

Infections

Garlic is a natural antibiotic and fungicide. (See *Earache*, *Sore Throat*, *Sinuses*, and/or *Toothache*.)

Scabies

Scabies are little red mites that live under your skin and lay their eggs. Scabies cause severe itching, particularly at night, and a red, pimply rash. Because of garlic's anti-parasitic qualities, it can be applied topically to kill off scabies.

Cut a fresh clove of garlic and rub it over your skin where the scabies are living, or crush garlic, mix it with a little olive oil, and spread the mixture evenly over the scabies-infested skin. Leave the garlic treatment on for one hour. Repeat until the scabies are gone, which may take up to ten days. Note: Scabies are different from the mites your pet might have.

Sinuses

Garlic can clear the sinuses. Sinus infections and nasal congestion can be combated with a garlic oil remedy.

Sinus Remedies

Drops—Press two cloves of garlic through a garlic press. Add forty drops of water from an eyedropper. Stir thoroughly and let the mixture settle. Fill the eyedropper with the clear liquid that rises to the top. Hold your head back and place ten drops of the garlic-water mix into each nostril. Sniff deeply and pinch your nose closed to keep the remedy from running out while you breathe through your mouth for two minutes. Blow your nose and begin to breathe normally.

Inhalant—Combine four crushed cloves of garlic and one teaspoon of apple cider vinegar in a large bowl. Add two cups of boiling water and inhale the steam and garlicky vapors as they rise from the bowl.

Skin

Garlic has proven helpful in clearing up persistent, flaky red blotches on both the skin and scalp. Dandruff, or itchy scalp, is often caused by a fungal infection and raw garlic's powerful antifungal properties can put a stop to scalp scratching. You can make a garlic dandruff lotion by combining the following in a glass jar:

- ½ cup vodka
- ½ cup distilled water
- one medium-sized crushed garlic clove

Secure the jar lid tightly and wait three days. Then strain the lotion to remove the garlic bits. Store the lotion in the glass jar with the lid on. Several times each week, moisten a cotton ball with the lotion, dab the lotion onto the scalp, and gently rub it in.

Garlic facial? Yes indeed! Garlic stimulates blood flow and can leave you with a healthy glow.

AUTHOR'S FIELD NOTE

I am not a nervous or anxious sort by nature, but during a recent case of deadline stress I developed an ugly red rash on my face. While researching garlic for this book, I uncovered the cure right in front me—you guessed it—garlic. I first tried cutting a clove and rubbing it on my face, but saw no effect. Then I crushed a clove into a small bowl, let it sit for ten seconds, and smeared it on my "problem area." Within twenty-four hours the redness had diminished, and in three days, it was completely gone. Crushed garlic clearly cured my own case of dermatitis!

Garlick maketh a man wynke, drynke, and stynke.
—THOMAS NASH, RELATIVE OF WILLIAM SHAKESPEARE

Sore Throat

Garlic can be used as a lozenge to fend off a cold, a sore throat, or even tonsillitis. Sucking on a raw clove of garlic may save you a trip to the doctor.

Stomach Problems

Raw garlic is helpful in killing off bad bacteria that might be festering in the gastro-intestinal tract and aids in digestion.

Stress

Stress causes the body to emit toxic substances into the bloodstream that can make even the best of us irritable, exhausted, and mad. Stress can give you indigestion, make you fat or thin (always the opposite of what you are hoping for), and mess with your blood pressure and blood-sugar levels. Garlic's almighty allicin will help you detoxify—it is a powerful antibiotic. Garlic lowers blood pressure and is also a mood elevator.

Toothache

If you have a dental disaster, crush garlic and spread it on and around the tooth or suck on a whole clove to ease the pain until you can get to the dentist. Ancient Greeks and Egyptians used garlic to fill cavities in teeth to prevent abscess and infection. You can do the same as an emergency measure. Garlic can also be helpful in treating gum infections and canker sores.

Toothache Remedy

Crush a clove of garlic and mix it with peanut butter. Apply the poultice to the aching tooth and leave it for some time until the pain eases.

Weight Loss

Garlic has been known to help satisfy hunger, as documented in the Talmud, the book of Jewish laws and traditions. Adding garlic to food can make the food more satisfying because garlic adds a lot of flavor and very few calories. Additionally, scientists believe that garlic can actually prevent weight gain. Laboratory rats that were given a diet high in sugar put on less weight if they were also eating garlic regularly.

Worms

Raw garlic is a vermifuge—that is, a botanical medicine that will kill worms living in the gastrointestinal tract of both people and animals. It will also kill the fungus more commonly known as ringworm (see *Fungus*). To get rid of unwelcome worms living on your plants, see *Insect Repellent and Pest Deterrent*.

Wounds

Garlic's natural germ-fighting power can help keep wounds free of infection—it is nature's pocket antibiotic.

"For me, a garlic grower, working in the fields with hammers and nails and shovels has given me my fair share of cuts and scrapes and bruises but I have not used ointments or salves or meds for them. I have rubbed all of my cuts and scrapes and bruises, no matter how serious, with raw garlic and sometimes I will do it several times. I have never had one infection."

—CHESTER AARON, FAMOUS AUTHOR AND GARLIC EXPERT,

WWW.CHESTERAARON.COM

Yeast

An overgrowth of yeast in the body can be responsible for ailments including athlete's foot, clogged sinuses, digestive upset, earaches, flatulence, food allergies, low blood sugar, migraines, thrush (yeast infection in the mouth), red and flaky skin, and vaginal and anal itching, to name a few. Garlic's anti-fungal properties help to adjust yeast levels to normal and maintain a healthy balance of yeast in the body.

Yeast Remedy

Eat one or two raw cloves, chopped, daily.

Gilroy

Garlic is grown commercially in more than 175 countries around the globe. When it comes to garlic growing in America, every alliophile (neologism for garlic lover) knows to follow his or her nose to Gilroy, California. Gilroy is about forty miles south of San Jose, and if you've never seen garlic growing on a grand scale, you must have a look—it is something that will change the way you see the produce on your plate, forever.

Gilroy has come a long way since the 1920s when the first, small garlic fields were planted there. Today, Gilroy grows an estimated eighty percent of America's entire garlic crop and is the center of America's large-scale garlic production and processing operation. Gilroy is home to Christopher Ranch, the largest U.S.-based garlic producer, processor, packer, and shipper. Check out the Christopher Ranch website *www.christopherranch.com* for their product lineup, recipes, garlic info, health tips, and a comparison between Chinese garlic and Christopher Ranch California-grown garlic.

Cooking a Steak in Gilroy

American humorist Will Rogers commented on the air in Gilroy, California during harvest season and claimed it was "the only town in America where you can marinate a steak just by hanging it on the clothesline."

Gilroy is also where 100,000-plus garlic lovers gather annually during the last weekend of July for the famous Gilroy Garlic Festival that was started in 1979 by Christopher Ranch owner Don Christopher. The Gilroy Garlic Festival is the largest garlic festival in the world today—it's all fresh garlic (about 6,000 pounds of it), all the time for three whole days. See *www.gilroygarlicfestival.com* for details.

It's no joke about following your nose to Gilroy. May through June is garlic harvest and curing season, and during that time the town literally stinks—or, looked at another way, smells like heaven.

AUTHOR'S FIELD NOTE

I earned my private pilot's license while living in the Silicon Valley and I can confirm that it reeks of garlic at 1,500 feet when the garlic is curing!

Growing Your Own

Garlic is one of the few garden plants that deer won't devour and is a good choice to grow at home—all you need is dirt, full sun, and some cloves of your favorite garlic. Garlic is easy to grow, and it seems to take hold almost everywhere—in pots on a rooftop, in raised beds, or in well-drained soil. In general, garlic thrives in climates with cold winters, but some varieties, such as Creoles, have adapted well to warmer climates. (Refer to *Varieties* for additional information.)

Garlic is usually planted in the fall and is then harvested in the summer, about nine months later. Once it has been harvested, it needs to dry and cure for a few weeks to develop its full flavor.

For big bulbs and best results, plant organic garlic cloves in the fall, a month or two before the ground freezes. Once planted, your garlic cloves immediately get to work establishing good, healthy root growth right away, without delay. Garlic has contractile roots that are optimized, not for nourishment, but rather for pulling the bulb down deeper into the ground for protection. This is one of garlic's clever self-preservation mechanisms. Garlic needs to spend time in the cold ground "digging in" and gathering up the strength it will need for spring.

Garlic may be good for you. But growing your own garlic may be even better.
—STANLEY CRAWFORD, *A GARLIC TESTAMENT: SEASONS ON A SMALL NEW MEXICO FARM*

If you can't start until springtime, growing garlic is still worth it, but don't expect big bulbs. Chances are you'll be hooked on growing your own and then you can spend the summer making plans to plant more garlic in the fall. Here are some basic steps to guide you from digging to dining:

- ▶ Ensure that plants have rich soil and good drainage to help to prevent fungus. Prepare the soil with compost or manure. Clay soil won't produce good results—the clove won't be able to expand into a bulb if it's growing in a straightjacket.

▸ Plan your planting—your garlic will grow to a height of 2.5 to 3 feet and the leaves need plenty of direct sun. Garlic plants don't have many leaves so each leaf has a big photosynthesis job to do—don't overcrowd. Space garlic cloves about five inches apart in a row and allow ten to twelve inches between rows.

▸ Plant firm, healthy, skin-on cloves one to four inches into the ground and don't use any cloves with any spots or blemishes. The garlic you grow will inherit the properties of the clove you plant, so choose wisely. If you are planting cloves direct from the bulb, break the cloves from the bulb right at the time when you are ready to plant so that the cloves don't dry out. This process is called "popping" or "cracking" and freshly popped cloves often have small roots ready to grow. Help them out! After 5,000 years of cultivation, garlic cloves have become smart enough to right themselves but, if you have the time, give your garlic a head start and plant the cloves skinny end up.

▸ Cover with a few inches of mulch, enjoy the winter, and be patient— good garlic comes to those who wait.

▸ In the spring, look for small, flat, green shoots that morph into flat leaves.

▸ Fertilize, weed, and mulch. Fertilize to add soil nutrients, and weed to remove anything other than the garlic plants so all nutrients are focused on the garlic. Mulch to keep the weeds from coming back be- cause each garlic leaf needs maximum sun. Mulching will also help to keep the garlic cloves safely tucked under a blanket of cool earth as they transform and grow into bulbs.

▸ Watch for plant overcrowding and, when the plants grow to be about fourteen inches tall, carefully pull out a few plants if necessary to provide ample space for the remaining garlic to thrive in the sun. But don't let the plants you pulled out go to waste—these are garlic

greens and can be eaten. You can even replant the garlic greens elsewhere. We put ours in clay pots and gave them as exotic, garlic garden
starter gifts once they've started to scape.

▸ If you've planted hardneck garlic, snap off the flower stalks as they
appear or just let them curl and go crazy. These are the garlic scapes
that can be eaten when they are young and tender.

▸ Determine when it's harvest time. It's time to harvest when at least
half of the leaves turn brown, wither, and droop. You can check the
size of the bulb by carefully pulling the dirt away with your hands
from the top of the bulb. Does it stay to grow, or does it go? If it
stays, be sure to cover it back up completely.

▸ When it's time to unearth them, loosen the garlic bulbs from the
ground with a pitchfork or shovel and then grab the plants by the
leaves and shake off the loose dirt. This is easiest to do if the ground
is dry. After the bulb has dried and cured, you will be cleaning it
again, so just brush off the loose dirt at this stage.

▸ Take a bulb or two of this fresh-out-of-the-ground vegetable and use
it in the kitchen. You'll discover that it is the drying and curing process that gives garlic it gusto.

▸ Dry and cure the garlic in a very dry, sunlight-free, well-ventilated
place until it is hard and firm. Tie the garlic plants in bunches of no
more than ten or twelve and hang them to dry or spread them out
on screens. Low moisture and good ventilation are critical for curing
because this keeps mold from wasting your work. Clean and trim the
bulbs—cut off tops, trim off the whiskery roots, and remove excess
dirt, but be sure to leave sufficient bulb wrappers intact to protect
the cloves and to maximize storage life.

▸ Store in a cool, dark, well-ventilated place.

▸ Enjoy and be sure to share your crop with friends.

"When I harvest my garlic I hang it (uncleaned) in an area that is protected from rain for 5–8 weeks. During that time, if I were to taste the different varieties, they would all come close to "tasting" alike. During those 5–8 weeks the stalks and bulbs will lose their water and they will weigh only half the weight they had when they were first hung. After hanging, and once the stalks and roots are cut, the taste differences are most profound. I have found that, for me, those taste differences will last for only two or three months. Then the different varieties taste more alike as time goes on."

—CHESTER AARON, FAMOUS AUTHOR AND GARLIC EXPERT,

WWW.CHESTERAARON.COM

Hygiene

Garlic can not only make you smell better—at least to people who like the smell of garlic—it can also contribute to your personal cleanliness in other ways.

Garlic Breath

Garlic breath is perhaps the *only* negative thing about garlic, but the many benefits of garlic may make the odor worth putting up with. Garlic breath is generally considered base and vulgar. In the days of Shakespeare, if a man's breath smelled of garlic or onions, it meant he was lower class— garlic and onions were staples of the working classes, peasant food.

If you have garlic breath, consider chewing on a few coffee beans or crunching some coriander seeds. These are both effective ways to neutralize garlic breath—although then, of course, your breath smells like coffee or coriander. Gum and mints will do their best to cover it up, but lingering odor depends on body chemistry.

Eating raw garlic produces the strongest garlic breath. Eating roasted garlic still offers many garlic health benefits, but leaves behind less pungent breath.

COOKING TIP

Use roasted garlic instead of raw garlic in recipes—it helps to curb garlic breath and adds a rich, nutty, rustic, roasted, delicate garlic flavor. Roasted garlic is a great way to introduce garlic to timid tasters.

Although today garlic breath is considered an acceptable by-product of many national cooking styles, the Japanese are possibly too polite to have garlic breath—traditional Japanese cuisine is one of the few in the world that does not use garlic.

Some people may recoil and gasp at garlic breath, but in the ancient world it was an important test of a woman's fecundity. In ancient Egypt and also in ancient Greece, according to Hippocrates, if a women's morning breath smelled of garlic after sleeping with a clove of garlic in her vagina, she was considered fertile.

Take Some Garlic on Your Date

Of course, some people just can't stand the smell of the stinking rose. Garlic breath can be conveniently used as a weapon to keep away unwanted advances of all kinds— man, woman, or vampire. Traditionally, of course, garlic repels the embrace of a vampire. In Bram Stoker's *Dracula* (1897), Professor Van Helsing hangs a wreath of garlic bulbs around the neck of Lucy Westenra to prevent Dracula from biting her (although in the end, the vampire gets her when her mother tears away the wreath—how's that for irony?).

Fingers magically lose their garlic smell when they rub against a stainless steel object such as a kitchen utensil or faucet. I thought that perhaps sucking on a stainless steel spoon would alleviate my garlic breath, but it didn't make a bit of difference. Removing the smell of garlic from the surface of the hands is a simple matter. However, once garlic is ingested, the garlic's essential oil passes into the blood and is aerated into the lungs. Because garlic breath is produced from within the body, no amount of spoon sucking would ever help. Garlic odor also escapes through the pores, but stainless steel can't help eliminate garlic body odor either.

GARLIC QUIZ: Garlic breath is hard to cover up. Which of the following will help your breath return to its normal condition after eating garlic?

1. Mints
2. Gum
3. Fresh parsley
4. All of the above

Answer: 4

International Cuisine

Garlic remnants found in the caves of ancient humans tell us that the plant has been pleasing the palates—even the most unrefined and unsophisticated of them—for a very, very, very long time.

And there was a cut of some roast . . . which was borne on
Pegasus-wings of garlic beyond mundane speculation.
—C. S. FORESTER, AUTHOR

Garlic comes into play in varying amounts in most regional cuisines around the world with only a few noteworthy exceptions. The British, the Scandinavians, and the Japanese stay away from the "stinking rose." The

United States of America, late to table compared to the rest of the world, uses garlic because it was an essential part of the nation's ethnically eclectic "melting pot." Those Americans unfamiliar with garlic despite their ethnic ancestors learned how to use it in the 1960s, largely thanks to chefs Julia Child and James Beard.

For additional information on garlic and its uses worldwide, see Chapter 3: *Garlic Across Cultures and Around the World.*

Joke or No Joke

Joke (for kids)

Q: What did the onion say to the garlic?

A: You stink.

No Joke (thankfully not enforced)

In Gary, Indiana it is illegal to go into a movie theater or to ride a streetcar within four hours of eating garlic.

No Joke (alas, no longer meeting)

"The Lovers of the Stinking Rose" fan club, or LSR for short, was America's first and only garlic fan club. Lloyd John Harris's pro-garlic goal in starting LSR was to promote and to protect garlic in the mid-1970s when garlic was less well accepted on American soil.

LSR membership entitled one to a copy of Lloyd John Harris's first book, *The Book of Garlic,* a lifetime subscription to the *Garlic Times* newsletter, and discounts on mail-order items sold through the book and newsletter. All this in Berkeley, California, well before the advent of the Internet.

If you'd like to sit in on a great meal with the LSR board of directors as they dine in Truckee, California, dust off your VCR and watch *Garlic's Pungent Presence* by Beacon Films Magic Lantern Productions. I was lucky enough to find it at my local library and it is now unlucky enough to be stuck inside the one and only remaining VCR in my neighborhood.

LSR is no more, but you can find Harris still stirring things up at *www .foodoodles.com*—he's still eating incredibly well and, yes, wearing that goofy, garlic, ceremonial toque! Visit the site and see for yourself.

Kitchen Tools

Here are a few of the basic kitchen tools you need when working with garlic:

Garlic Press

If there is one, single kitchen gadget that is essential for great garlic gastronomy, it is the garlic press. Here's how it works. The garlic clove, peeled or unpeeled, is placed into a small well with tiny holes in the bottom. The clove is crushed and forced through these small holes when the plunger is pressed down over the clove. Cleaning is easy if it is done before the garlic dries in the holes. Too late and it's all plugged up? Soak the garlic press in hot water to soften the garlic jam. Some presses come with a tool for easy cleaning, but a toothpick does the trick as well.

Although you'll find a handful of garlic presses on the market, the best and only garlic press you'll ever need to purchase is one of the easy-to-clean, dishwasher-safe, Swiss-made Zyliss garlic presses. There are two Zyliss models and both are cheaper, easier to use and clean, and far better clove crushers than the more expensive models because the holes are optimized for steady extruding.

The smaller Zyliss press, the Susi Garlic Press, was awarded the honor of "Best Garlic Press" by the *New York Times* and *Cook's Illustrated* and costs around $15. The larger model, the Zyliss Jumbo Garlic Press, lets you press multiple cloves at the same time and is in the $20 price range. Both Zyliss models are relentless workhorses, able to press unpeeled cloves of garlic with a single-handed squeeze. Both come with a five-year manufacturer's guarantee.

There are five elements: earth, air, fire, water, and garlic.
—LOUIS DIAT, AUTHOR

Garlic Peeler

The E-Z-Rol Garlic Peeler, designed by retired Playboy Club architect Ben Omessi and now sold by Zak Designs, is a dishwasher-safe, flexible rubber tube that resembles manicotti. Place the E-Z-Rol Garlic Peeler on the counter, tuck a few fresh garlic cloves into the cylinder, and roll it back and forth with the palm of your hand. Presto! The E-Z-Rol pulls on the garlic skin and pops it right off of the cloves, leaving the cloves whole and unblemished.

Garlic Chopper

This might seem to be overkill, especially if you've got a garlic press, but if you want diced garlic that's not smashed or crushed, this gadget will do the trick. Place the garlic on top of the cutting grid and bring down a metal mesh of tiny blades that dice the clove for you. Choppers run anywhere from $4 to $18. You can also find a garlic chopper with a set of rolling metal blades that will slice and dice the garlic any way you want.

But at the end of the day, when working with garlic nothing beats the power of a good chef's knife, honed to a razor sharpness.

Love

Make love smothered in garlic? Well, some of us would certainly consider it. Read on.

Aphrodisiacs and Adultery

Garlic has long been considered an aphrodisiac. Aristotle named garlic on his list of aphrodisiacs. Roman historian and naturalist, Gaius Pliny the Elder (23–79), recommended garlic pounded with fresh coriander and red wine as an aphrodisiac.

As well, its smell could be used to disguise illicit hanky panky. The Greek playwright Aristophanes wrote of cheating wives who bathed in garlic oil and ate garlic before their men returned home from duty in order to cover up the smell of their transgressions.

King Henry IV of France (1553–1610) was known as a very kind and compassionate king. He was also infamous for his abundant, complicated, amorous affairs and for his many mistresses. He was obsessed with demonstrating his virility and his sex appeal, despite the fact that he had several beautiful wives, successfully managed multiple mistresses simultaneously, carried a cathouse VIP pass, and possessed the power to have his way with any woman he winked at. He proved to be truly insatiable. In order to keep it all up, he used garlic as his special tool. In the end he was assassinated— stopped only by the knife.

Love Potion Number Nine: Garlic

A true potion, as opposed to a tonic, for example, is a concoction that has an immediate miraculous, magical, and medicinal effect upon the person who ingests it, whereas a tonic is taken routinely over time to strengthen and fortify the body gradually. Garlic is a key ingredient in both tonics and potions, and has been used to instigate *amour* throughout the ages.

In ancient Palestine, a groom wore a clove of garlic on his shirt to ensure a successful wedding night.

The Talmud of the ancient Hebrews includes instructions on using garlic to improve circulation, cure jealousy, and encourage love. It recommends eating garlic on Fridays, the traditional Hebrew night of the marital bed.

Garlic is as good as ten mothers.
—ANCIENT TELUGU PROVERB FROM INDIA

Music

"Music" is the name of a delicious, medium-hot, rocambole (hardneck garlic) that is a proven performer in colder climates. The music we mention here, however, is of the vocal, folk variety.

"The Garlic Waltz," also referred to as "The Garlic Song," was written by Ruthie Gorton (now Rutthy Taubb) and was featured in the movie *Garlic Is as Good as Ten Mothers* in 1980. This amusing song was more recently performed and recorded by Claudia Schmidt and Sally Rogers on their *While We Live* album. Its allium-centric lyrics are listed here:

The Garlic Waltz

Words and Music by Rutthy Taubb

There are spices and vegetables that you can grow,
Some are under the ground, some grow tall,
Though they all have their qualities, this you should know,
That the garlic is best of them all.
You can use it in poultry, in fish, and red meat,
Or to spice up a vegetable stew,
In fact, it improves everything that you eat,
And it serves as a medicine too.
Since Biblical times, in all parts of the earth,
It has cured countless sufferings and ills,
If we understood what the garlic is worth,
We would throw out our poisonous pills.
The Egyptians, Phoenicians, the Vikings and Greeks,
Babylonians, Danes, and Chinese,
On their voyages took enough garlic for weeks,
And their enemies died on the breeze.
In Bulgaria's mountains and Russia's wide plains,
People live to a hundred years old,
For it's juice of the garlic that runs in their veins,

Oh it's worth twice its weight in pure gold.

With selenium, germanium, allicin too,

It can fight off all types of disease,

So if you've got arthritis, T.B., or the flu,

Just say, "Peel me a garlic clove, please."

Plant some cloves in your garden to keep away worms,

And the other bad things that kill plants,

If you're one of those people concerned about germs,

You can drop one or two in your pants.

There are spices and vegetables that you can grow,

Of all colors and shapes, large and small,

After going through this, I am sure you must know,

That the garlic is best of them all.

How I Came to Write "The Garlic Waltz"

By Rutthy Taubb (formerly Ruthie Gorton)

I'm not sure what year it was, but it was in the 1970s that I received a call from my friend Les Blank. He was making a film about garlic and wondered if I would write a song about it to help raise money to finish the film. There was going to be a fundraising dinner at Chez Panisse in Berkeley, California and he wanted me to sing my song about garlic at the dinner.

I'd always written by inspiration and never on assignment so I accepted the challenge, hoping I could do it. I went to the health food store and bought a book called *The Miracle of Garlic* by Paavo Airola, which was all the inspiration I needed. I had always loved garlic but I didn't know enough about it to write a song until I read that wonderful book.

After writing the song, I went to Berkeley and sang at the dinner at Chez Panisse, which had garlic in every course from garlic soup to garlic ice cream. We got to see the part of the film that was finished and raised enough money to help Les finish *Garlic Is as Good as Ten Mothers*. I got to sing my song in the film in four-part harmony, thanks to the miracle of recording technology.

If you are reading this book, you must love garlic. If you haven't seen that film, I highly recommend it before dinner because it will make you very hungry. That reminds me of another little story. When Les came to Los Angeles to show his film at the Fox International Theater in Venice, California, he had garlic roasting in the toaster oven at the back of the theater during the film. You can imagine the sensory overload. Of course, we ate the garlic after the film.

Nicknames

Garlic, known formally as *Allium sativum*, has garnered many different nicknames over the ages. There is one thing, however, that all of these various nicknames have in common. All of garlic's nicknames are based either on its natural power as a healer or on its severely sulfurous stench. Garlic has been called:

- Bronx Vanilla
- Chinese Penicillin
- Cholesterol Buster
- Earth Apple
- Essential Ingredient
- Halitosis
- Indispensable Ingredient
- Italian Marijuana
- Italian Perfume
- Mother Nature's Underground Pharmacy
- Nature's Most Versatile Medicinal Plant
- Nature's Super Healer
- Poor Man's Viagra
- Pungent Plaque Attacker
- Russian Penicillin
- Rustic Treacle (a treacle is an ancient remedy taken to counteract a poison)
- Stinking Lily
- Stinking Rose
- The Cure-All

- ▸ The Great Healer
- ▸ The Spice of Life
- ▸ The Stinky Savior
- ▸ Vitamin G
- ▸ Wonder Drug of the Herbal World

Botanists have held, and still do, different opinions when it comes to formally classifying and naming individual members of the allium family. As a result, another nerdy nickname for garlic is allium controversum. Very funny!

Numbers

Think of the fish we used to eat free in Egypt, the cucumbers, melons, leeks, onions, and garlic.
—NUMBERS 11:5, KING JAMES VERSION

0 The number of scapes that rise up from a softneck garlic plant

1 The number of scapes that rise up from a hardneck garlic plant

1 The number of organic garlic cloves it takes to start your own crop

1 The number of cloves in a single serving of garlic

1 The number of teaspoons of minced garlic that equal one medium clove of garlic

2 The number of pounds of garlic eaten per person in the United States in 1996

3 The weight, in grams, of a single clove of garlic

3 to 12 The number of months a bulb or head of garlic stays fresh when kept cool (not cold), dry, and away from sunlight

$3.99 The average cost per pound of softneck artichoke garlic at the grocery store today

4 The number of calories per clove of garlic

4 The number of French thieves who concocted and donned "Four Thieves Vinegar" to avoid the plague while robbing the dead to get filthy rotten stinking rich

4 to 40 The number of garlic cloves in one bulb or head of garlic—hardneck garlic has far fewer cloves than softneck garlic

6 The minimum number of times a bulb of garlic is handled by the time you buy it

8 to 10 The percentage of the annual garlic yield that growers put back into the ground to produce next year's crop

10 The number of garlic cloves not to exceed daily if you wish to avoid the danger of an allergic reaction

10 The percentage of garlic that is grown worldwide in comparison to onions

10 The number of hardneck garlic varieties

10 The number of seconds it takes for garlic to activate its powerful healing agents after it is crushed, cut, or chopped

13 The percent of refuse in a bulb or head of garlic, i.e. the knob and skin

40 The number of cloves in the dish made famous by James Beard and Julia Child: Chicken with Forty Cloves of Garlic

42 The weight of the largest bulb of garlic, in ounces, as recorded by the *Guinness Book of World Records*

75 The percent of the world's garlic that is produced by China

175 The number of countries growing garlic

377 The tariff percentage that the United States has levied on garlic imports from China to protect domestic growers

400 The amount of fresh garlic, in millions of pounds, sold annually in the United States

555 The weight of garlic, in millions of pounds, that was grown in the United States in 1997. As a point of comparison, 140 million pounds were grown in the United States in 1975.

4608 The grocery standard, 4-digit PLU (Product Look-Up) code assigned to garlic. By industry convention, organic produce is assigned a PLU code with a leading 9 placed in front of the non-organic, 4-digit PLU code. Organic produce is assigned a 5-digit PLU code.

94608 The grocery standard, 5-digit PLU (Product Look-Up) code assigned to organic garlic. The leading 9 indicates an organic product.

My final, considered judgment is that the hardy bulb
[garlic] blesses and ennobles everything it touches—
with the possible exception of ice cream and pie.

—ANGELO PELLEGRINI, *THE UNPREJUDICED PALATE*

Nutrition

Garlic is exceptionally good for you because of its powerful and complex chemistry as outlined throughout this book. The following basic nutritional information comes from the USDA and is the starting point from which the power of garlic emanates.

Although this list is lengthy, each item is uniquely unremarkable. But great things begin to happen when just a single clove—one serving—is crushed.

Garlic Nutrition Facts
Amount Per Serving
Serving Size 1 clove (3.0 g)

Proximates

- Water 1.76 g
- Energy (calories) 4 kcal
- Protein 0.19 g
- Total lipid (fat) 0.01 g

- Ash 0.04 g
- Carbohydrate .99 g
- Fiber 0.1 g
- Sugars 0.03 g

Minerals

- Calcium, Ca 5 mg
- Iron, Fe 0.05 mg
- Magnesium, Mg 1 mg
- Phosphorus, P 5 mg
- Potassium, K 12 mg
- Sodium, Na 1 mg
- Zinc, Zn 0.03 mg
- Copper, Cu 0.009 mg
- Manganese, Mn 0.050 mg
- Selenium, Se 0.4 mcg

Vitamins

- Vitamin C, total ascorbic acid 0.9 mg
- Thiamin 0.006 mg
- Riboflavin 0.003 mg
- Niacin 0.021 mg
- Pantothenic acid 0.018 mg
- Vitamin B6 0.037 mg
- Choline, total 0.7 mg
- Vitamin K (phylloquinone) 0.1 mcg

Lipids

- Fatty acids, total saturated 0.003 g
- Fatty acids, total polyunsaturated 0.007 g
- Cholesterol 0 mg

Amino acids

- Tryptophan 0.002 g
- Threonine 0.005 g
- Isoleucine 0.007 g
- Leucine 0.009 g
- Lysine 0.008 g
- Methionine 0.002 g
- Cystine 0.002 g
- Phenylalanine 0.005 g
- Tyrosine 0.02 g
- Arginine 0.019 g
- Histidine 0.003 g
- Alanine 0.004 g
- Aspartic acid 0.015 g
- Glutamic acid 0.024 g
- Glycine 0.006 g
- Proline 0.003 g
- Serine 0.006 g

Ornamentals

They look like overly large lollipops or fantastic fireworks frozen on a stick, and they're cropping up in gardens everywhere these days. They resemble a dried dandelion dramatically poised for a big blow, but they're ornamental alliums. They are, like garlic, another incredibly impressive—however inedible—member of the allium family. And like garlic, there are hundreds of them.

Although all alliums are perennials, you won't find these garlic relatives among the perennial plant picks at the garden center or nursery. Ornamental alliums, like garlic, are grown from bulbs and they are planted in the fall so that they can crop up in the spring. You'll need to plan and plant ahead.

And now that you know a thing or two or three or more about garlic, you'll probably notice that the ornamental allium resembles the hardneck garlic with its single, attention-getting scape, and its largely unattractive, withery leaves.

My Rochester, New York neighbor is well known for her dramatic family gardens and is a great neighborhood source of gardening wisdom and practical know-how. She and her gardening followers have been ordering their alliums for years direct from Colorblends in Bridgeport, Connecticut. Call them at 1-888-847-8637 or visit their website *www.colorblends.com* to browse through their online catalog or to request that a printed copy be mailed to you. Colorblends's allium bulbs have produced stunning allium displays each and every year. You'll also find many other online bulb catalogs to choose from. The following are popular alliums that come recommended. They are listed in order from shortest to tallest:

- *Allium caeruleum*: 12–18 inches tall, produces a blue globe of only 1 inch in diameter, blooms late spring to early summer.
- *Allium christophii* (a.k.a. Star of Persia): 12–18 inches tall, produces a shiny, purple globe of about 6–10 inches in diameter, blooms early to mid-summer.
- Allium "Globemaster": 24–36 inches tall, produces a violet globe of about 10 inches in diameter, blooms late spring to mid-summer.
- Allium "Purple sensation": 30–36 inches tall, produces a purplish-red globe of about 4 inches in diameter, blooms late spring to early summer.
- *Allium giganteum* (a.k.a. giant allium): 36–48 inches tall, produces either a white or a purple globe of about 6 inches in diameter, blooms late spring to early summer.
- Allium "Gladiator": 48–60 inches tall, produces a rose-colored globe that is about 6–9 inches in diameter, blooms late spring to early summer.

Prepared Garlic

Modern living is full of convenient timesavers, and prepared garlic is one of them. It comes in many forms and is a handy shortcut if you don't have fresh garlic on hand, but usually only if it will be cooked. Prepared garlic is particularly helpful when you need large quantities of garlic in a hurry and you are pressed for time. But if you are making a salad dressing, or if you want to toss some raw garlic into a pasta dish or into some butter for garlic bread, don't use prepared garlic unless you absolutely have to. Of course, it's all a matter of taste, but for the best flavor, you'll want to use fresh garlic. Don't believe it? Try it and see for yourself—it's not that much work, and a bulb of fresh garlic will keep for months. (See *Storing*.)

Because prepared garlic is usually better than no garlic at all, grocery stores carry prepared garlic in many convenient forms. Prepared, raw garlic comes in jars of peeled, whole cloves, slices, chopped, crushed, or minced garlic, garlic juice, and pureed garlic in a convenient toothpaste-like tube. Prepared, dried garlic products are all made from dehydrated garlic that is ground to size. Garlic is rarely frozen because freezing makes the garlic flavor disappear.

Prepared Raw Garlic Products

On those occasions when you must use prepared garlic, here are some things to be aware of:

- ▶ Prepared, raw garlic products can last a long time, thanks to chemical preservatives and refrigeration. Fresh minced garlic, on the other hand, will stay flavorful for only a few hours and then become bitter.
- ▶ Commercially produced garlic in oil must contain preservatives such as phosphoric or citric acid in order to be sold in the United States.
- ▶ Garlic preserved in oil also needs to be refrigerated for freshness because there is a very real risk of botulism food poisoning, so read the label and know the symptoms. Symptoms of botulism food poisoning include blurred or double vision, speech and breathing difficulty, and progressive paralysis.

Prepared Dried Garlic Products

Dried garlic products include chopped garlic, garlic flakes (a.k.a. instant garlic), garlic powder, garlic granules, ground garlic, minced garlic, and garlic salt. These are all dehydrated garlic that is ground to specific consistencies, plus moisture-absorbing agents. Garlic salt contains a tiny amount of garlic powder and a whole lot of salt.

Dried garlic products are best used in meat rubs and are not a satisfactory substitute for fresh garlic. All that said, refer to *Cooking with Garlic* for equivalents that just might help out in a pinch.

Qualities of Specialty, Gourmet Garlic

What qualities make specialty, gourmet garlic so great?

1. Clearly it's quite fresh.
2. The quintessential garlic flavor is an important factor. (See *Tasting* for details.)
3. Unquestionably the number of unique varieties is key. For information on the varieties of garlic, see *Varieties*.

But specialty garlic is so much more than freshness, taste and type. Here are a few of the remarkable things that I discovered during my quest for specialty, gourmet garlic:

▶ It was a huge thrill to know exactly where my specialty garlic came from. When I ordered from Vanderpool Gourmet Gardens online via Gourmet Garlic Gardens, I used Google Maps to take a look at Texas and saw the farm and the very garlic fields where my garlic had been grown. Now that's a good use of technology!

▸ I found great satisfaction in communicating directly with the farmers who grew, harvested, cured, labeled, and shipped my garlic. It was clear that these farmers treasure unique garlic crops, and they took the time to describe the varieties of garlic they shipped and to label each bag carefully.

As an entrepreneur myself, the fact that my garlic was grown on an independent, family farm pleased me immensely. The farmers all believe they are growing something healthy and wonderful that is best when shared.

▸ I also loved the personal anecdotes that the farmers sent via e-mail or tucked into the boxes, and I was fascinated to learn about the history of a few of the garlic varieties. One of the e-mails is shared on the following page. These personal touches made me treasure my garlic even more and made it seem magical somehow. And it made for great dinner discussion.

Specialty, gourmet garlics are magnificent, culinary jewels that are downright beautiful. They come in different colors, shapes, sizes, and textures. They look simply fantastic!

Once you've seen, touched, and tasted a few different varieties of specialty, gourmet garlic, you'll get it. Visit your local farmers' market or connect directly with garlic growers online. See Chapter 6: *Garlic Getaways and Essential Resources* to get started today.

My order via *www.gourmetgarlicgardens.com* was shipped direct from Vanderpool Gourmet Gardens in China Spring, Texas.

Trina,

Following is a list of the garlic I am sending for your order. I tried to give you a broad variety with some very rare garlics and diverse, but excellent, flavors.

    Texas Rose: see note below
    Red Toch: artichoke
    Lorz Italian: artichoke
    Inchelium: artichoke
    Spanish Benetee: creole
    Burgundy: creole
    Music Pink: porcelain
    Sonoran: turban
    Maiskij: turban
    Vekak: glazed purple stripe
    Duganski: purple stripe
    Siberian: marbled purple stripe

Texas Rose: this is a very early heirloom garlic from Halletsville, Texas, 30 or so years earlier from Mexico. Anton J. Bujnoch, Sr. has been growing this garlic for 30 years or so. His sister Emma brought it from northern Mexico during a hunting trip there. It was apparently left on a table in a hunting lodge by locals. It is a very distinct garlic in the way it grows and how early it harvests, earlier than even the turban varieties. Its flavor is very nice, and the coloration of the bulb wrappers is rare in garlics that look like this. It appears most closely related to artichoke varieties, but seems different enough that it may be genetically distinct from that group. After receiving some of this garlic last year from Bob Anderson, I tracked down the source and found the Bujnochs. I went directly to them and got the history of the garlic and purchased several pounds. They called it "garlic," but due to its distinct history, color, and uniqueness, I call it Texas Rose.

Please let me know if you have any questions.

Sincerely,

Terry Vanderpool

Vanderpool Gourmet Gardens
254-640-4054

Relatives

If you take a quick look at the Allium Sativum Family Tree in Chapter 1, you'll likely discover that you already know many of garlic's closest culinary relatives. These edible alliums are essentially garlic's fragrant brothers and sisters—they all fall directly under the genus Allium. If you're a gardener in search of garlic's more decorative and dramatic kin, see *Ornamentals.*

Chinese Chives

The Chinese chive (*Allium odorum* and *Allium tuberosum*) is a hearty perennial with flat, edible, garlic-tasting leaves, and clusters of delicate, white flowers that shoot up in late summer on top of a 20-inch seed stalk or scape. Chinese chives are also known as garlic chives and used in Chinese as well as in Japanese cooking to add a delicate, garlic flavor.

Chives

The chive (*Allium schoenoprasum*) is a hearty perennial with delicate, smooth, tube-like, edible leaves. Chives are typically minced and used as a culinary seasoning, as a salad green, or are sprinkled on top of a dollop of sour cream on top of a hot baked potato. Chives are easy to grow in pots, and they are both edible and colorful in that they send up round, pink or lavender blossoms that are 1 to 2 inches in diameter. They are a popular pick for the deck or rooftop gardener. Chives are short—they typically grow no more than 12 inches tall.

Elephant Garlic

Elephant garlic (*Allium ampeloprasum*) is sometimes called great-headed garlic and, in spite of its name, it is really a leek. It is relatively mild in taste and can grow to be as big as an orange and weigh up to a pound or more! It is not uncommon for the elephant garlic bulb to consist of one, single clove or "round," instead of individual cloves. Elephant garlic sends up a seed stalk or scape, and it even produces a seedpod full of white flowers, but it does not produce bulbils, the little mini cloves within the seedpod—like a hardneck garlic does.

Garden Onions

The garden onion (*Allium cepa*) is also known as the bulb onion or the common onion. It is a biennial plant that is typically harvested in its first year. The garden onion has long, hollow leaves that resemble scallions, and it produces edible, underground onion bulbs in hundreds of colors, shapes, and sizes—yellow onions, white onions, red onions, Spanish onions, boiling onions, pearl onions, Vidalia onions, and Walla Walla onions, to name a few of the 700 varieties that you probably already know. Like garlic, once onions have been harvested, they need to dry and cure before they are ready to eat. The onion produces powerful, healing sulfurous compounds when the bulb is cut and, like garlic, onions have been used in folk medicine since before recorded history.

Leeks

The leek (*Allium porrum*) is a biennial, with thick, broad leaves and a thick white bottom. As a biennial, leeks need two years to complete their full growth cycle but they are at the peak of their flavor in their first year, which is when they are harvested. Usually only the white, bottom part of the leek is used in cooking because the green leaves tend to be bitter. Leeks are used most commonly in soups, but they may also be braised and served as a side dish.

COOKING TIP

Even if they appear clean and ready to use on the outside, leeks are more than likely filled with hidden dirt and grit because they are repeatedly covered up with extra soil as they grow to keep them white. This process is called "hilling." To clean a leek thoroughly, slice it in half once the long way and soak it in water in an oblong pan prior to using. It's surprising how much dirt and grit will escape.

Scallions

Scallions (*Allium fistulosum*) are sometimes called green onions, spring onions, Japanese bunching onions, or Welsh onions. Scallions have broad, hollow, tube-like green leaves and marble-sized, white bulbous bottoms. Like leeks, scallions are biennials that are grown as annuals—they are harvested in their first year when they are tender and tasty. Both parts of the scallion—the bulb and the leaves—are edible. Scallions are commonly used in Chinese cooking.

Shallots

The shallot (*Allium ascalonicum*) is a robust perennial whose bulb adds a delicate onion flavoring to sauces. It is a prized favorite in French cooking. Like garlic, a shallot bulb is comprised of individual cloves—it looks more like a brown, bronze, or purplish parchment-wrapped garlic bulb than an onion.

COOKING TIP

Three to four shallots can be substituted for one medium-sized onion.

Ramps

Ramps (*Allium trioccum*) are also known as wild leeks or ramsons. Ramps grow wild in shaded woods and in mountainous ravines as far north as Nova Scotia, Canada, as far west as Minnesota and Iowa, and as far south as Georgia. They are best known for growing wild in the hills of North Carolina and Tennessee and, like garlic, ramps are celebrated with annual spring ramp festivals and down-home Appalachian neighborhood gatherings. Ramps resemble scallions with flat, long leaves and a white or reddish stalk that ends in an exaggerated, long white bulb. Ramps have a strong onion flavor and all parts of the ramp are edible.

Religion

Whether or not you believe the legend that Satan left behind one onion-growing footprint and one garlic-growing footprint as he fled the Garden of Eden, the fact is that garlic exhibits such extreme effects on *Allium sativum* eaters themselves, and on the people that they encounter, that religious rulings were warranted.

Mohammed (570–632), founder of the religion of Islam, despised the smell of allium breath and forbade followers from entering mosques if they had eaten garlic or onions.

Buddhist monks, as well as Jain and Hindu religious leaders, must refrain from eating both garlic and onions because of the offensive, residual body odor and also because garlic encourages intimacy and other impure thoughts that lead to bad behavior.

The Jews, however, go great guns for garlic *because* it encourages intimacy. Michael Caduto's, *Everyday Herbs in Spiritual Life: A Guide to Many*

Practices examines food, faith, and health in many cultures and describes the Jewish tradition as noteworthy for being "rich in beliefs and practices related to food, faith, and community." The Talmud is the ancient document that lays down the laws and customs of the Jewish people around the world. It specifically prescribes eating garlic on Friday night, the traditional night of the marital bed.

Well loved he garleek, oynons, and eek lekes. And for to drinken strong wyn, reed as blood.
—GEOFFREY CHAUCER, POET

Storing

Fresh garlic is best stored in a cool, dry, well-ventilated place and away from direct sunlight. But don't put it in the refrigerator. In the fridge, garlic will sprout because cold gets garlic growing!

If your garlic is in plastic when you bring it home, remove it pronto so the bulb can breathe. Just like you, garlic is a living wonder that needs air to do its job right and to fulfill life's expectations. Put your garlic in a basket, in a clay or stoneware garlic keeper with air holes (available at most cookware stores), or in a shallow, open bowl. The main idea is to keep your garlic in the dark, to keep it cool, and to ensure that the air can circulate. Don't keep it in a closed container.

Whole, fresh garlic, stored properly, should last for months, but the exact length of time depends upon the variety of garlic and how it was handled prior to arriving at your house. Softneck garlic varieties have a longer storage life than hardneck varieties, and this is one of the reasons why it is more common in most grocery stores.

Once the bulb is broken open, storage life decreases, which is why it is important to buy whole bulbs with at least a few bulb wrappers that are fully intact. Properly stored, it can be kept up to two months before the cloves are too shriveled up to produce a good garlic flavor. But once broken from the bulb, cloves are at their best for only up to ten days.

Supplements

If you'd like to tap into garlic's powerhouse of natural health benefits but don't like the taste of garlic, don't want to risk smelling like it, prefer not to cook, can't get your hands on fresh garlic, can't take it with you, if garlic doesn't like you . . . or if you simply like the convenience, accuracy, and precision of pills and prepared foods, consider garlic supplements. They offer an easy, effective, and sometimes odor-free way to get your daily dose.

Garlic supplements are one of the most popular, natural health preparations on the market today. They help people of all ages with health concerns such as heart disease, high blood pressure, high cholesterol, and diabetes to get their GQ (garlic quotient) effortlessly without the kitchen work, and frequently without the odiferous aftermath. Ask around— you might be surprised to find out who's taking garlic supplements right under your nose.

Popular Choices

The most popular supplement choices are garlic oil, garlic powder capsules or pills, and aged garlic extract. Choosing the right garlic supplement is tricky because much can be lost in the manufacturing process, because it is difficult to label effectiveness consistently, and because garlic starts working once it is inside the body and can't be measured at all. Not to be bamboozled by this and determined to understand garlic supplements so that I could summarize their importance and provide the at-a-glance essentials here for you, I pulled the following books out of my towering stack of garlic references and studied them closely:

- ▸ *For the Love of Garlic: The Complete Guide to Garlic Cuisine* by Victoria Renoux
- ▸ *Garlic in Health, History, and World Cuisine* by Susan Moyers
- ▸ *Garlic: Nature's Original Remedy* by Stephen Fulder, PhD and John Blackwood
- ▸ *Garlic: Nature's Super Healer* by Joan Wilen and Lydia Wilen
- ▸ *Healing Power of Garlic* by Paul Bergner
- ▸ *The Healing Benefits of Garlic* by John Heinerman
- ▸ *The Natural Pharmacist: Natural Treatments for High Cholesterol* by Darin Ingels

You'll find more information on these great garlic references in the *Bibliography* and *References* section of this book. Read up because the garlic supplement information is vast. You may want to concoct your own garlic remedies. If that's the case, *The Healing Benefits of Garlic* and *Honey, Garlic & Vinegar Home Remedies and Recipes,* listed in the *Bibliography* and *References* section, both include recipes for making garlic ointments, potions, lotions, teas, gargles, inhalants, poultices, and syrups.

Here's a summation of information about garlic supplements:

▶ No one seems to understand fully garlic's magnificent healing powers, how garlic actually does it, and how it all works inside the body. It is a garlic power conundrum.

▶ Garlic supplements are popular today because staying healthy is easier than treating disease. Staying healthy is a lot less expensive and a lot more fun, too.

▶ People take garlic supplements today primarily to fend off heart disease, that is, to lower cholesterol, reduce blood pressure, thin the blood, prevent blood clots, and reduce the risk of atherosclerosis.

▶ Garlic supplements are all beneficial, however those that contain or allow allicin to form have the greatest antibiotic and antibacterial qualities.

▶ Companies who manufacture and distribute garlic supplements want you to choose their particular garlic supplement over the competition's and so they present their information accordingly. It is downright confusing.

Ask around, get advice, do your research. Take the time to investigate different supplements and gather information independently. The information can be conflicting and confusing, so seek professional advice from a nutritionist or doctor. And don't dismiss using garlic in the kitchen—eliminate the confusion and the middleman.

You probably won't be able to determine which product offers the most health benefits simply by comparing garlic supplements because no one knows for certain—the power that garlic unleashes in your body once it is ingested cannot be effectively measured. However, it is a fact that raw garlic, particularly freshly crushed raw garlic, is the strongest and most powerful form of garlic.

Garlic Pills and Capsules

Garlic pills and capsules are made from garlic powder, and they stay fresh for up to a year because the garlic inside them is dehydrated. Enteric coatings are used so that the pills dissolve in the intestines and not in the stomach. This helps minimize garlic breath and also ensures that the stomach acids don't interfere when garlic's alliin and alliinase blend to create allicin. The creation of allicin is what sets the rest of garlic's medicinal magic in motion and generates its powerful sulfur compounds. Allicin is the most powerful antibiotic component of garlic, yet some very effective garlic supplements contain no allicin at all. These supplements get their powers from garlic's sulfur compounds instead.

Aged Garlic Extract

Aged garlic extract is made by taking whole, sliced, or chopped cloves of garlic and soaking them in an extracting solution of alcohol for up to two years. This process removes the allicin and makes the resulting aged garlic extract truly odor-free. Kyolic is a popular brand name for aged garlic extract that is essentially odor-free. Because it has no allicin, some people believe that aged garlic extract cannot possibly be as effective as other supplements that have retained garlic's allicin. However, in spite of the fact that it is allicin-free, and in spite of the fact that Germany's Commission E would not allow aged garlic extract to be sold as a cholesterol-lowering supplement because of this, aged garlic extract has proven to have many, but not all, of garlic's health benefits. It has retained garlic's post-allicin powers to fend off heart disease by lowering cholesterol, lowering blood pressure, reducing blood sugar levels, and preventing the formation of blood clots that can lead to heart attack and stroke. Where aged garlic extract falls short, however, is in its ability to act as an antibiotic. Nor is aged garlic extract as effective a cancer fighter or immune system stimulator as fresh garlic.

Garlic Oil

Garlic oil was the original European commercial garlic product that was produced in the 1920s. Today, garlic oil has proven to have few of garlic's cholesterol-curbing components and is generally not as helpful in reducing cholesterol as other garlic supplements. The process of creating garlic oil removes both alliin and allicin, and the smell is so intensely garlicky that it is often cut with vegetable oil so it is tolerable and won't irritate the stomach. As a result, the amount of garlic oil in the capsule is too small to be effective. All this said, many people find garlic oil capsules helpful. Another example of the garlic power conundrum.

Since garlic then hath powers to save from death,
Bear with it though it makes unsavory breath.
—SALERNO REGIMEN OF HEALTH, TWELFTH CENTURY

Standardized Herbal Extract

Although most experts agree that fresh garlic offers the greatest number of healing powers, even the health benefits of fresh garlic vary from head to head. The medicinal power of garlic, as with many healing herbs, depends on many factors: genetics, where and how the plant was grown, the soil, how the plant was harvested and cured, how it was stored, etc. This makes a comparison of supplements particularly difficult because one clove of garlic may be very different from another. To overcome this and to provide consumers with a consistent measure of comparison, a "standardized herbal extract" has been defined. Many manufacturers of garlic supplements standardize either on the allicin content or on the alliin content to provide one or two points of comparison among garlic supplements. One of the complexities of standardizing on allicin content is that many of garlic's therapeutic qualities come from much more than allicin alone—garlic's cancer fighting and immune system bolstering qualities come from the enzymes and sulfides that are created within minutes after allicin itself breaks down. Standardizing on alliin content gives no indication of how much allicin is produced.

Healing Powers and Garlic Components

This list describes garlic's healing powers along with some of the preparations and the chemical components of garlic providing them. Note that all forms of garlic fight cancer, stimulate the immune system, detoxify, and lower cholesterol.

Although the components do not exist in all forms of garlic, this list can prove helpful in evaluating garlic supplements to determine which ones might best meet your needs. In a nutshell, garlic's allicin and allicin-related compounds act as antibiotics and blood thinners, and they lower blood sugar; garlic's sulfides and sulfide-related compounds act as antioxidants to protect against cancer and aging, and also lower blood sugar; garlic's ajoenes and dithiins act as antibiotics and as blood thinners; garlic's other components act as antioxidants.

Antibiotic

(Strongest in fresh chopped garlic, garlic powder, fresh garlic juice, garlic juice aged three to twenty-four hours, and fresh macerated garlic oil aged three to thirty-six hours.)

- Ajoene
- Allicin
- Allyl methyl thiosulfinate
- Diallyl trisulfide
- Methyl allyl thiosulfinate

Detoxifier

- Ajoene
- Aliin
- Allicin
- Allixin
- Allyl mercaptan
- Allyl methyl trisulfide
- Diallyl disulfide
- Dimethyl disulfide
- Dimethyl trisulfide
- Dipropyl disulfide
- Methyl ajoene
- S-allyl cysteine

Cancer inhibitor

▶ Ajoene
▶ Allicin
▶ Allixin
▶ Allyl mercaptan
▶ Allyl methyl trisulfide
▶ Diallyl disulfide
▶ Diallyl trisulfide
▶ Diallyl sulfide
▶ Propyline sulfide
▶ S-allyl cysteine

Antioxidant

(Strongest in fresh chopped garlic, garlic powder, cooked garlic, fresh garlic juice, garlic juice aged three to twenty-four hours, fresh macerated garlic oil aged three to thirty-six hours.)

▶ Aliin
▶ Cysteine
▶ Diallyl heptasulfide
▶ Diallyl hexasulfide
▶ Diallyl pentasulfide
▶ Diallyl tetrasulfide
▶ Diallyl trisulfide
▶ S-allyl cysteine

Lowers Blood Sugar

(Strongest in fresh chopped garlic, garlic powder, cooked garlic, fresh garlic juice, garlic juice aged three to twenty-four hours, fresh macerated garlic oil aged three to thirty-six hours.)

- ▸ Allicin
- ▸ Allyl propyl disulfide
- ▸ S-allyl cysteine sulfoxide

Lowers Cholesterol

- ▸ Ajoene
- ▸ Allicin
- ▸ Diallyl disulfide
- ▸ S-allyl cysteine

Thins Blood

(Strongest in fresh chopped garlic, garlic powder, fresh garlic juice aged three to twenty-four hours, fresh macerated garlic oil aged three to thirty-six hours.)

- ▸ Ajoene
- ▸ Allicin

Protects the Liver

- ▸ Diallyl trisulfide

Tasting

Now here's an idea to spice up your next gathering of real friends—a garlic tasting! A formal garlic rating and tasting might seem like an incredibly odd idea at first. It might even seem like a suggestion that stinks, but don't be too quick to dismiss this unusual opportunity to dig deeper into garlic—it just might grow on you. Wines do not look or taste the same. Nor do apples, lettuce, grapes, and pears—or garlic. Who knew? But now you do.

Dressed Up for Garlic

If you really want to have fun, suggest to your friends that they dress formally for the tasting, just as they might for a high-class wine tasting.

The fact is that there is a lot to learn about garlic and considering that you are now well-read enough to know that there are two subspecies and ten varieties of *Allium sativum*, it just might be time to gather your friends and teach everyone a thing or two.

The First Tasting

The first formal garlic rating and tasting ever recorded took place on Bastille Day, July 14, 1981, at the Chez Panisse restaurant in Berkeley, California. Lloyd John Harris, founder of the garlic club "Lovers of the Stinking Rose," publisher of *The Garlic Times* newsletter, and author of *The Official Garlic Lovers Handbook* details how eight varieties of garlic were rated on six dimensions using a garlic-rating scale created expressly for this premier event.

This pioneering team of garlic aficionados and self-proclaimed alliophiles (garlic-lovers) rated the physical characteristics of whole garlic bulbs, unpeeled cloves, peeled cloves, and sliced cloves. They tasted and rated baked bulbs and raw cloves while using sangria as a palate cleanser and snacking on basic bread and plain butter with a simple side salad and fresh corn on the cob.

Looking over accumulated tasting notes, garlic has been evaluated on these dimensions:

Raw Garlic Tasting

▶ Fragrance

▶ Heat or piquancy: how hot it is

▶ Heat start: how long it takes the heat to hit

▶ Heat end: how long it takes the heat to dissipate

▶ Flavor

▶ Intensity of garlic flavor (not the same as heat)

▶ Aftertaste (sometimes afterburn!)

Roasted Garlic Tasting Dimensions

▶ Appearance

▶ Fragrance

▶ Taste

▶ Texture

Chester Aaron, author, garlic grower, and garlic expert, lives in the California wine country and has become the leading expert on conducting formal garlic tastings. He's provided some tips and suggestions for us:

Garlic Tastings

Whenever I host a garlic tasting, I set out a pattern of bowls. For each of the garlic varieties to be tasted, there is a set of two bowls. One is a bowl of fresh hummus dip with a dash of olive oil; the other is a bowl with the same amount of fresh, raw, pressed garlic. The garlic variety used to prepare the hummus dip is the exact same variety that is presented in the bowl of raw garlic. They are teamed together.

For each garlic variety, in front of each set of bowls, I place a slip of paper that identifies the variety of garlic with as much information as I can collect about that specific variety.

People will taste the garlic and then they will debate over which garlic has the stronger garlic taste and which has the stronger garlic aroma. They will try to determine which garlic is hotter, which is milder, which is richer, which is tasteless, which hits you where—lips, tongue, back of the throat, etc. They take it very seriously, like they are judging fine wines!

But it seems that everyone has a different opinion. The reason opinions differ is because each of us has different body chemistry. What might be hot for me can be mild or even tasteless for you.

Garlic that is freshly picked is quite mild in taste, whereas garlic that has been dried and cured has a sharper taste.

White-skinned garlic with small cloves is sharper than garlic that has a purplish tinge.

Set a date in the fall: The best time to plan a garlic gathering is August to October when you are more likely to find different varieties of fresh garlic at local farmers' markets. If your goal is to taste different kinds of garlic, you will want to be sure that you can get your garlic before setting a date.

Get your garlic: If one of your goals it to sample different varieties of fresh garlic, chances are that you'll need to get your garlic somewhere other than your local grocery store. Go to a local farmers' market or look online for organic growers. Getting a number of varieties of garlic to taste may be the trickiest part of the preparations, but if you use the online farmers' market contacts provided in Chapter 6 of this book, you can have your garlic delivered to your doorstep. Timing is key here because fresh garlic goes quickly and does not keep long. When you find it, buy it. If for some reason you can only find one variety of garlic, simply change the goals of your garlic gathering—you can still learn and share a lot about garlic.

Invite your friends: Invite enough food-loving friends to fill your dining room table and then some. Choose people with a sense of culinary adventure.

Set some goals: Determine what you'd like to do with garlic at your gathering. Based on the garlic you are able to gather, some options are provided here:

1. Explore how different types of whole fresh garlic look and handle as they are prepared for cooking—compare softneck and hardneck wrapper colors, textures, and finishes. Then compare how the bulbs open, the color of the cloves, and how easily they peel.

2. Compare how different types of fresh garlic taste—explore the differences among various kinds of hardnecks (be sure to include a rocambole). Use a plain old grocery store silverskin or artichoke softneck as a traditional point of reference.

3. Learn how different one kind of garlic smells and tastes based on how it is handled and prepared—i.e., present a whole head, whole cloves, peeled cloves, chopped cloves, minced cloves, and crushed cloves.

4. See how many ways you can enjoy garlic in a single meal. This approach is more work for the cook, requires less participation from guests, and is iffy on the amount of garlic knowledge it imparts, but it is undeniably another great reason to host a feast.

5. Learn what's really in the various kinds of prepared garlic that your guests probably already have in their pantries (garlic powder, granulated garlic, minced garlic, garlic salt) and compare it with fresh garlic—it could change cooking habits considerably.

**It is not really an exaggeration to say that
peace and happiness begin, geographically,
where garlic is used in cooking.**
—X. MARCEL BOULESTIN, CHEF

Tasting notes and supporting materials: It's useful to provide a framework to help your testers know what to look for, taste, and take notice of. Provide pens and pencils along with notepads or prepared rating sheets with the tasting dimensions plus the names of the garlic varieties or dishes to be sampled. If you have time and are technically inclined, your laptop or tablet computer can even support you in these entertaining and educational efforts. Grab some pictures of garlic to create a poignant PowerPoint presentation. You can even display one of the narrated garlic flashcard sets for free at quizlet.com—or make your own if you have time.

Party decorations and favors: Go all out with garlic for this special occasion and use it all over. Depending upon the season, good garlic can be very hard to find, so if you are fortunate enough to hit the jackpot and find some great hardneck garlic, stockpile it and don't be even a little embarrassed about it. Buy enough bulbs to use for your rating and tasting activities and for the cooking you have planned. Then get more garlic so you can fill up big bowls to use as party decorations (mix with fresh lemons or limes). Getting even more garlic will allow you to send folks home with some of their favorite varieties as appropriately themed party favors. And grab some more garlic if you wish to make garlic-themed place cards to tell people where to sit or what they're about to dish up. Print names on small pieces of paper, fold them over a toothpick, stick them together with tape (or use a Post-It note), and then place the toothpick firmly into the stem of a whole bulb of garlic as the name cardholder. Ta dah—is there anything garlic can't help with?

AUTHOR'S FIELD NOTE

One of the highlights of my *A Miscellany of Garlic* odyssey was corresponding with author and garlic guru Chester Aaron. When my first box of gourmet garlic was enroute from Vanderpool Gourmet Gardens, I wrote to Chester and gave him the list of artichoke, creole, porcelain, turban, purple stripe, and glazed purple stripe garlics that would soon be mine: Texas Rose, Siberian, Red Toch, Lorz Italian, Inchelium, Spanish Benitee, Burgundy, Music Pink, Sonoran, Maiskij, Vekak, and Duganski.

Here is what Chester sent back to me. God love him!

TRY THIS!

1. Take 1 bulb of each of 4 different varieties of garlic.
2. With a very sharp knife, take a slice off the top of the bulb, cutting the tips off every clove and exposing the interior meat.
3. Loosen and free the cloves of each bulb (keep the bulbs separate so you don't mix the cloves up).
4. Place the cloves of each variety on separate flats of aluminum foil (large enough to fold up and over to enclose the cloves).
5. Pour, over each collection of cloves, 1 tablespoon olive oil and salt and pepper to taste.
6. Fold aluminum foil up and over the cloves.
7. Using a felt-tipped pen (a Sharpie?) write on the foil of each collection of cloves the name of the variety of the bulb those cloves came from.
8. Place aluminum-wrapped cloves (on an oven-safe platter) into a 400-degree oven.

9. Roast for 1 hour.
10. Bring out bulbs, unfold aluminum, and serve.
11. Cloves can be eaten and chewed and sucked free of flesh separately to experience different qualities of each of the 4 (or 5 or 6 or 7) varieties, that is, if there *are* different qualities.
12. No matter. Your garlics, roasted this way, will be delicious and offer a beautiful new experience around your table.
13. Appetizer? Dessert? Reward for skipping the martini?
14. Listen to the different reactions.

And more than all, how many of us have dined at the Réserve at Marseille, that famous restaurant on the Mediterranean shore, where the brothers Roubion have acquired immortal fame? There is but one word in English which describes the sensation of the traveller who eats there for the first time—that word is revelation. New truths seem to be imparted to you as you swallow, new objects and new theories of life seem to float around you. Strange ideas come to you across the sea: and when it all is over, when with a calm-bringing cigar, your legs stretched out, you silently digest and think, with the Chateau d'If and the flickering waves before you in the moonlight, you gratefully thank Providence for having led you there. All this is the effect of garlic, which works upon you like haschisch.

—*FRENCH HOME LIFE,* 1873

Umbel

Umbel is the formal name of the exotic-looking seedpod that grows on the end of a hardneck garlic scape or flower stalk. Refer to the hardneck garlic diagram in Chapter 1.

Only hardneck garlic varieties are fertile and therefore only hardneck garlics produce a scape and an umbel. This is often referred to as the "ability to scape." Softneck garlic is infertile and therefore has no need to produce a scape or an umbel, so it doesn't bother with the fanfare. Softneck garlic has lost its ability to scape—it is an extreme case of Mother Nature's powerful, evolutionary "use it, or lose it" mechanism.

The hardneck garlic's umbel is sometimes referred to as an "umbel capsule" or topset before it has fully developed and before the smooth spathe leaf that protects it pops open to display a very crowded mix of garlic flowers and garlic bulbils. Bulbils look like miniature garlic cloves and, when planted, they will produce a normal-sized head of garlic within a few years. Bulbils are only one of the three ways that garlic can be propagated. For more information on garlic's sexual and asexual reproduction, see *X-Rated*.

Varieties

As charted out in the Allium Sativum Traditional Family Tree, cultivated garlic, *Allium sativum*, is broken down into two basic types or subspecies: softneck and hardneck. There are more than 300 varieties of garlic in the world today. Some of them are described here:

Softneck Garlic

Softneck garlic (*Allium sativum*, subspecies sativum) is sometimes referred to as Italian garlic, Egyptian garlic, silverskin, and artichoke garlic (due to its artichoke-like clove structure). There are two varieties or cultivars of softneck garlic: artichoke and silverskin.

Softneck garlic is the most common type of garlic. Produced en masse around the world, it is the only garlic most of us have tasted and is the only garlic found in most grocery stores. It is the easiest type of garlic to grow, cure, transport, and store, and it typically produces more cloves than hardneck garlic.

Softneck garlic is infertile in that it produces no seed stalk or scape—it is "scapeless." It is therefore sometimes referred to as non-bolting garlic and it is grown directly from a clove.

Softneck garlic may yield up to twenty-four cloves per bulb, in three to six layers. It produces an outer ring of large cloves and several inner clusters of smaller, sometimes comically tiny, sliver-like cloves.

Softneck garlic is the subspecies of garlic that is most commonly found woven into decorative garlic braids because it is scapeless and easy to manipulate at harvest time.

Main softneck garlics with brief descriptions follow:

Artichoke—the most common of the larger, grocery store garlics, with medium to large bulbs, mild flavor, three to five clove layers generally, and twelve to twenty cloves per bulb; bulb wrappers are coarse with a matte finish, white with a purple tinge; it grows well in temperate climates without severe winters, and keeps six to nine months.

Among the many varieties or cultivars of artichoke garlic you'll find Blanco Piacenzo, California Early, California Late, Chamiskuri, Chet's

Italian Red, Chilean, Early Red, Inchelium Red, Italian, Kettle River Giant, Loiacono, Lorz Italian, Lukak, Machashi, Madrid, Okrent, Olomuk, Oregon Blue, Polish White, Purple Cauldron, Red Toch, Sicilian Artichoke, Siciliano, Simonetti, Susanville, Thermadrone, Tochliavri, Transylvanian, Trueheart Tzan (Mexican Red), Viola Francese, and Zahorksy.

Silverskin—the most common small to medium-sized garlic in grocery stores, teardrop shape, it has the longest storage life of all garlics (up to one year); smooth, shiny, pure white bulb wrapper, with three to six clove layers; it generally tastes hot when used raw, and tastes best when minced and sautéed.

Among the many varieties or cultivars of silverskin garlic you'll find Idaho Silver, Locati, Mexican Red Silver, Mild French, Nootka Rose, Prim, Rose du Var, S&H Silver, Sicilian Silver, Silver White, St. Helens, and Wedam.

The quality and taste of a particular variety of garlic can depend on many factors such as the soil of the growth area, the weather where it was grown, when that garlic was harvested, how that garlic was cured, and how long after the harvest that particular garlic was used for cooking or tasting.

—CHESTER AARON

Hardneck Garlic

Hardneck garlic (*Allium sativum*, subspecies opioscordon) is sometimes referred to as stiffneck, topset, topsetting, or serpent garlic.

Hardneck garlic is usually found only at local produce stores and farmers' markets in the summer and fall. Look in Chapter 6 for online farmers' markets so you can purchase direct from the growers across the United States, which is precisely what we did in preparation for this book.

Hardneck garlic is currently considered to be a specialty, gourmet garlic. As its name implies, it has a hard neck that is brittle and difficult to bend. This neck itself is the telltale sign for determining the kind of garlic in hand. The hard neck is actually the base of the garlic scape, which is the long shoot that snakes and coils as it grows, producing the seedpod, also called an umbel or a spathe, which is full of bulbils. The bulbils are tiny garlic cloves that can be planted, but they take two to three years before they grow to become a normal-sized garlic bulb.

Hardneck garlic typically produces between four and fourteen cloves per bulb, formed in a single circle around the hard neck. The cloves are usually easier to peel than softneck cloves.

There are eight varieties or cultivars of hardneck garlic. The most common types of hardneck garlic are described here:

Asiatic—when growing, the umbel (seedpod) has an extraordinary, long "beak," purple bulbils, and may have brown, deep red, or purple cloves with thick skins, often with purple stripes on the bulb wrapper; leaves are yellow-green and wide, and it's ready to harvest when only a few leaves are brown.

Here are a few varieties or cultivars of Asiatic garlic: Asian Tempest, French Red Asian, Pyongyang, Russian Redstreak, Sakurai, and Wonha.

Creole—also called Mexican Purple, it grows great in hot, southern climates and does not grow well in climates with severe winters; scapes bend but do not coil; its generally small bulbs, with white or pinkish-purplish bulbils, may have more than one ring of cloves; it has great taste and can taste sweet or hot, keeps well, and is good-looking with red or purple clove skins.

Here are a few varieties or cultivars of creole garlic: Ajo Red, Burgundy, Creole Red, Labera del Obispo, Manuel Benitee, Morado de Pedronera, Pescardero Red, Rojo de Castro, and Spanish Benitee.

Glazed Purple Stripe—rounded, oval-shaped cloves, with shiny, metallic-looking silver and purple bulb wrappers, sometimes bulb wrappers have bronze or gold tones; rich flavor.

These are a few varieties or cultivars of glazed purple stripe garlic: Blanak, Purple Glazer, Red Rezan, and Vekak.

Marbled Purple Stripe—grows best in regions with severe winters and early, warm springs, but is known to grow extremely well in hot climates, too; bulbs have purple stripes or patches and large, fat cloves that are sometimes brown or purple; it stores well, is easy to peel, and tastes hot when consumed raw.

Among the many varieties or cultivars of marbled purple stripe garlic you'll find Bai Pi Suan, Bogatyr, Brown Tempest, Brown Vesper, Bzene, Choparsky, Duganskij, Jovak, Khabar, Metechi, Monshanskij, Northe #3, and Siberian.

Porcelain—handsome, usually with white satiny bulb wrappers that sometimes have purple or copper-colored streaks; big fat bulbs with four to six big fat cloves; it grows well in cold climates with severe winters, making it a popular variety grown in Canada, but it can adapt to growing in warmer climates; sensitive to soil conditions just before harvesting and needs moister soil than other hardnecks; scapes must be cut or bulb size is greatly reduced; although it's the largest garlic plant with the largest cloves, the umbels contain the smallest bulbils; hard to peel; stores well; has the highest concentration of allicin and associated health benefits.

Among the many varieties or cultivars of porcelain garlic are Armenian, Blazer, Fish Lake #3, Floha, Georgian Crystal, Georgian Fire, German White, Kyjev, Lapanantkari, Leningrad, Majestic, Music, Music Pink, Polish Hardneck, Romanian Red, Rosewood, Russian Giant, Susan Delafield, Vostani, Wild Bluff, Yampolskij, Yugoslavian Porcelain, Zaharada, and Zemo.

Purple Stripe—eight to twelve cloves, with vivid purple stripes on clove skins and bulb wrappers; grows well in regions with severe winters and in poor conditions; genetically closest to the wild *Allium sativum* species; scapes must be cut or bulbs will be small; strong and complex taste, not sweet; regarded as best for roasting; cloves can be thin-skinned and difficult to peel; stores well.

Among the many varieties or cultivars of purple stripe garlic are Belarus, Duganski, Ferganskij, Red Grain, Samarkand, Shatili, Shvelisi, Skuri #2, Tien Shan, and Vercnjaja Mcara.

Rocambole—sometimes called "serpent garlic" this best-known, most popular, and most available hardneck has six to eight cloves and dull, boring, off-white bulb wrappers, occasionally with purple stripes or purple tinge; a chef's favorite, rich and sweet, finest tasting of all garlics, it makes the best salad dressing, and is the one to choose when garlic is the main, featured ingredient in a dish; requires cold winters, grows well in regions with severe winters, and does not grow well in hot climates; tends to grow "double cloves" and has the curliest scape of the them all, which should be removed or bulb size is reduced; blue-green leaves; limited storage life (three to six months); easy-to-peel skin.

Many varieties or cultivars of rocambole garlic exist including Baba Franchuk's, Belgian Red, Brown Saxon, Carpathian, German Brown, German Red, Killarney Red, Maxatawny, Montana Giant, Montana Roja, Ontario Giant, Pitarelli, Rocambole Music, Russian Red, Spanish Roja (a.k.a. Greek or Greek Blue), Vietnamese, Wisconsin German Red, Youghiogheny Purple, and Yugoslavian.

Turban—nicknamed the garlic world's "summer apple" it has the shortest dormancy and should be harvested early when only a few leaves are brown; tastes hot when consumed raw, very mild when cooked, often used more like a vegetable than a spice; has blotchy purple or purple-striped bulbs, typically slender tan or pink cloves; droopy scapes need not be removed because they do not affect bulb size; harvest quickly so bulb wrappers don't deteriorate.

The many varieties or cultivars of turban garlic include Blossom, Chengdu, China Stripe, Chinese Pink, Chinese Purple, Dushanbe, Lotus, Luster, Maiskij, Red Janice, Shandong, Shilla, Sonoran, Thai Fire, Uzbek Turban, and Xian.

A little garlic, judiciously used, won't seriously
affect your social life and will tone up more dull
dishes than any commodity discovered to date.
—ALEXANDER WRIGHT, AUTHOR

Garlic and War

A proven, natural antibiotic that's easy to transport and store, garlic was used in ancient times to successfully disinfect wounds and to treat the battle injuries of fallen Greek and Roman warriors.

During World War I, garlic was also used to treat the wounded, to prevent gangrene, and to cure dysentery, a severe and sometimes fatal gastrointestinal disorder.

Marching right along, during World Wars I and II, garlic earned the nickname "Russian penicillin" for its stellar performance in Russian regimes and for treating respiratory infections in hospitals.

Let me tell you about my own experience as a combat soldier in WWII. We, the Americans, had penicillin and ointments but the Russians did not. I would see Russian soldiers, when wounded, pull garlic cloves right out of their pockets and rub the garlic on their wounds.
—CHESTER AARON

Physical wounds are one thing and garlic has proven to be a great healer. Economic wounds, on the other hand, cannot be treated with the "super bulb"—even when the war is all about garlic itself.

In the mid-1990s, the United States instituted a 377 percent tariff on all garlic imported from China in an effort to protect the U.S. garlic growers against garlic "dumping" by the Chinese. China was busy selling fresh garlic to the United States at LTFV (less than fair value) and was driving smaller American garlic growers out of business. Nicknamed "The Garlic War" by the media, the fight against Chinese garlic dumping is still going on today, but now the war has expanded beyond the United States. The war is raging in Europe, as well. From December 2010 to January 2011, six containers holding 317,465 pounds of stealth Chinese garlic were cleverly disguised as onions to avoid the European Union's ad valorem duty. The European Anti-Fraud Office (OLAF) intercepted the garlic in Poland.

X-Rated

Garlic's potent power as an exceptionally effective aphrodisiac has been held in high esteem since before written history. But the X-rated subject of our discussion here has nothing at all to do with you and human sexuality. We're talking about down-in-the-dirt garlic sex for garlic's own reproductive sake. Garlic is largely asexual and therefore thinks nothing of it, but you might. If you're garlic, you can reproduce in one of three, yes, count them *three*, different ways depending on the reproductive structures you choose to use, if they still work.

The first kind of kinky thing about garlic's sex life is that most garlic plants are sterile, which means that they are no longer capable of producing fertile flowers or true seed. They've become asexual. So if you're a gardener looking to grow garlic, stop looking for seed packets—you'll never find them. Proceed to method #1 following, because it's the favorite way for garlic to reproduce: cloves. You can simply start your garlic garden with a head of garlic from your very own kitchen cupboard.

Method #1:
Asexual Reproduction by Means of Cloves

Hardneck and softneck garlic's universal, favorite, and easiest method of reproducing is by means of cloves, and yes, size matters. Large cloves tend to produce large bulbs so pick and plant accordingly. Cloves are garlic's easiest-to-tap-into reproductive structures and cloves are programmed to grow into a bulb that is an exact replica of the clove's main "mother bulb." Some growers refer to it as garlic's "memory." Freaky. Carefully break the cloves off of the main bulb in October or November just prior to planting, and push them into the ground. They can dig in before the frigid winter comes and then spring into action when the earth begins to warm. In June or July, what was once a single clove has become a multi-cloved clone of the original bulb and is ready to do it again.

The Garlic Seed Foundation in Rose, New York is a well-established educational resource for garlic growers and you can visit them online at *www.garlicseedfoundation.info*. However the primary "seed" they are referring to is Method #1: Asexual Reproduction by Means of Cloves. It's the easiest and most popular way for garlic to reproduce without sex, and without exception.

Method #2:
Asexual Reproduction by Means of Bulbils

The second method of garlic reproduction is by means of bulbils, and this is exclusive to hardneck garlic varieties. By now you probably know that softneck varieties have no seed stalk or scape (hence the name softneck), no seedpod, and therefore no bulbils to do it with. Only hardneck garlic sends up a seed stalk or scape that produces a seedpod that botanists call the plant's "inflorescence." When the inflorescence opens up, it is full of flowers and the tiny bulbils that are like miniature garlic bulbs. The tiny bulbils can be planted and do eventually grow into good-sized bulbs, but it takes a few years and isn't a very common method of intentional garlic reproduction. Most garlic growers snap off the scapes before the inflorescence even forms, in order to allow the plant's energy to be focused on growing one big garlic bulb instead of tiny flowers and bulbils.

Method #3:
Sexual Reproduction by Means of Seed

If you're garlic, reproducing by means of seed is truly "the wild thing" because only wild garlic plants are capable of doing this and it is very, very, very rare. Modern-day garlic has evolved to be infertile—it lost its ability to produce viable seed and fertile flowers thousands of years ago. Garlic's amazing ability to adapt to any environment has enabled it to survive and to reproduce asexually, entirely on its own. However, in 1986 a few fertile primitive garlic strains were discovered on the northwestern side of the Tien-Shan Mountains in central Asia. These garlic strains are being studied closely and are believed to be the closest living relatives of the original garlic. This quite possibly could be the precise area where garlic originated. Carefully orchestrated laboratory experiments have only just recently produced garlic seed from the wild garlic strains that originated in central Asia. Only a few wild varieties of garlic are capable of reproducing sexually by means of true seed.

Yoshio Kato

Yoshio Kato is famous for taking traditional Japanese folk medicine's garlic footbaths, ointments, and poultices to what might seem like an extreme level.

Yoshio Kato developed a unique, totally garlic-focused medical therapy and treatment that he named Flow-Leben therapy. In German, the word *Leben* means "life," and this Zen-like, total therapy system reflects Kato's holistic approach to his garlic treatments. He believed, researched, and demonstrated that life could be greatly improved and that illness could be cured when garlic was flowing through the body.

He was introduced to the healing power of garlic at a young age when the juice of a single clove saved his life. This inspired him to devote his entire life and his entire career to harnessing the power of garlic, in order to help others overcome debilitating diseases.

Total Garlic Therapy

Flow-Leben's total garlic therapy system involves daily doses of raw garlic. Additionally, Flow-Leben patients:

- Sit in a hot sauna to open the pores of the body;
- Take a garlic shower in a patented Flow-Leben machine that injects a prepared garlic solution into all the pores of the body;
- Shower with cold water to close the pores;
- Lie still for at least half an hour while a fairly thick covering of grated garlic is applied to the infected or affected areas of the body;
- Rinse.

Yoshio Kato's garlic treatments have cured more than 15,000 formerly "incurable" patients. His book, *Garlic: The Unknown Miracle Worker: Odorless Garlic Medicine and Garlic Flow-Leben*, was released in 1973. The book describes Kato's detailed garlic preparations. He summarizes the five curative applications of garlic or methods as follows:

1. Eat raw, grated garlic.
2. Eat garlic preserved in miso.
3. Apply raw, grated garlic to your ailing body part(s).
4. Apply a peeled garlic clove to your affected body part(s).
5. Gargle with the juice from grated garlic diluted with water.

The book also includes testimonials and dosages for using the above garlic methods to cure stomach, heart, and liver ailments, paralysis, tuberculosis, pneumonia, tonsillitis, asthma, skin disorders, skin cancer, frostbite, ringworm, alopecia, and constipation.

With garlic, the patient himself is doctor, pharmacologist, nurse, and pharmaceutical manufacturer all in one.

—YOSHIO KATO

Garlic in Your Own Yard

Your very own yard can benefit from garlic. Even if you have only a slightly greenish thumb, you might want to grow edible or ornamental garlic in your yard for fun. You can also protect your plants with garlic by tossing some cloves around the base of trees, plants, and shrubs to say "keep away" to deer, rabbits, and the rest of the night-chew crew. Garlic spray makes a great, natural insect repellent that repels mosquitoes and kills pests, mold, and fungus on your plants. Chances are also very good that you can find great garlic growing on a large scale in your proverbial "own back yard."

The Urban Gardener

Garlic is a good choice for the urban garden because it is likely to survive an onslaught of unwelcome garden invaders—wild animals and insects stay away from garlic. Garlic proves to be the last plant devoured by deer, gophers, woodchucks, groundhogs, moles, and the other stealth, urban vermin that seem to be set on destroying the fruits—and the vegetables—of every honest gardener's labor.

> ► You can do it! Because garlic is designed to survive in the harshest of climates and with the shoddiest of care, it can adapt and grow in practically any environment. This means that garlic is likely to make a gardener out of you yet—it is easy to grow, hearty, and drought tolerant. See *Growing Your Own* for step-by-step getting started tips for edible garlic growing at home. Cloves are typically planted in the fall and spend the winter digging in. Harvest time is early to mid-summer. See *Ornamentals* for information on those big,

whimsical, lollipop-looking alliums—you can plant them in the fall to make your flowerbeds really pop next spring and summer.

▶ Garlic requires very little attention for the vigilance it offers. Plant a protective garden border of garlic using either the understated edibles or the impressive, eye-popping ornamentals. Garlic spells, or rather smells, "keep out" to nosy noses and is a deterrent that can protect the jewels of your inner garden.

▶ In her book *Roses Love Garlic: Companion Planting and Other Secrets of Flowers*, author Louise Riotte describes how planting garlic within a flower garden protects against insects and even enhances the fragrance of the flowers themselves. As the book title implies, garlic is particularly good planted alongside roses. It protects against mildew, fends off black spot, and repels moles. Mole repelling seems to run in the family because daffodils, another popular member the liliaceae family, also discourage them.

Insect Repellent and Pest Deterrent

Insects avoid garlic, which makes garlic a natural, safe, and effective pest repellent. As it grows, garlic keeps insects away from other plants. You can also mix garlic in water to create an effective homemade insect repellent and garden spray. Treat individual plants with it to protect them from hungry predators. Here's how to make your own:

1. Combine a dozen or so cloves of fresh garlic with a cup of water and mix thoroughly in an electric blender or in a food processor.
2. Strain the mixture through a fine sieve or through cheesecloth into a bowl or measuring cup in order to remove any garlic chunks. Reserve

the liquid insect repellent concentrate and discard the garlic chunks, or sprinkle them around the border of your garden to deter all enemies.

3. Add three to five drops of liquid dish detergent, hand soap, or vegetable oil to the liquid insect repellent concentrate so that it sticks more easily to the plant leaves.

4. Store the insect repellent concentrate in the refrigerator in a glass jar with a tight lid. Label the jar clearly so you don't accidentally toss it when you clean out the fridge (yeah, right!) or mistake it for a savory something.

5. When ready for use, dilute the insect repellent concentrate with water, ten parts water to one part repellent.

6. Pour the insect repellent into a spray bottle and spray it on the tops and undersides of the plant leaves to protect them.

If you're not a DIYer, you can find natural insect repellents that include garlic oil at your local home and garden center.

A Garlic Growing Adventure

Are you looking for a local, healthy, fun, eye-opening, and edible adventure that the whole family can enjoy? Chances are pretty good that you'll find garlic growing on local farms and garlic being celebrated "in your very own backyard," so to speak. We sure did, and have included some entries from our "garlic log" here. Go to your local farmers' market and don't be shy— look around, and ask. That's what I did, as you'll see. Also, take a look in Chapter 6 of this book to see what garlic festivals and garlic growers are near you. Use the online resources listed and any others that you find to discover who's doing what with garlic in your particular area.

June 7—Local Green Garlic

Went to Rochester Public Market looking for fresh garlic for the book. No fresh garlic but found one farmer selling fresh "green garlic" (a.k.a. garlic greens). Many vendors had imported garlic from China. Bought one bunch of the farmer's garlic greens for $1.50. Chopped one of the greens up and put it in our dinner salad. The bulb was flavorful but the leaves were fibrous and tough. Enough garlic greens. Planted the rest in pots and put a few in Mom's flowerbed by the garage. Who knows, we'll see.

June 25—Some Local Scapes

Went back to Rochester Public Market for garlic gathering again. My online orders have begun to arrive but still want to see the locally grown stuff. No fresh garlic today, only a few farmers selling garlic scapes. We tasted a scape that was grown in a garlic field somewhere in Rush. The farmer would not say exactly where. Colleen bought a basket of scapes to put in her stir fry. I'm holding out for the bulbs.

July 2—Lots of Local Scapes

Back again to Rochester Public Market—book deadline pending, need fresh, local garlic. No fresh garlic but lots of fresh garlic scapes for sale—proof that hardneck garlic is growing somewhere around here.

July 16—Local Hardneck Garlic at Last

Back to Rochester Public Market again and finally—Eureka!—I found it! Only Louie Bell and Anita Amsler, who work together as a farming team, had fresh, hardneck garlic bulbs for sale. I picked it up and marveled at it. "German Hardneck," Louie offered up with a big, proud smile. I bought it, thanked him, admired his radishes, got brave and said, "I know this sounds crazy but I'm writing a book on garlic and I'm trying to find some garlic fields here in Rochester so I can include some pictures of it growing."

"Ours is all picked and hanging in the barns to cure," he replied.

"That would be even better," I replied sort of awkwardly. Then, before I knew it, I had Anita's name and her phone number on a small scrap of paper in my pocket. Another dream come true on my garlic odyssey! I was thrilled and they could tell.

July 18—Amazing, Local Garlic Adventure

An unforgettable day in many ways—the first morning rain in at least seven weeks, Sarah (Sally) Strong Clapp's memorial service, full sunshine upon exiting Third Presbyterian Church, a wonderful celebration in her honor, and the highlight of the year so far—a trip with Jack and Nancy to a farm in Walworth, New York, where garlic grows just twelve miles from my childhood home!

Anita and Louie are neighbors and make a great, self-appointed, farming team. They currently plant three varieties of garlic: Music, Italian Softneck, and German Hardneck. Theirs is a sustainable farm and they confess that growing garlic is a lot of work done by hand. But hard work does not frighten either one of these kind, vibrant, blue-eyed farmers; they clearly love their work, keep meticulous records, and they are powered by the egg sandwiches that Louie's wife sends down with Louie every day for lunch. Because Anita and Louie save their own garlic "seed" (it's really cloves, as you know by now) and did not need to buy new garlic seed to plant for next year's garlic harvest, they escaped the devastating "bloat nematode" disease that has recently caused many farmers to lose their entire garlic crops.

There are many miracles in the world to be celebrated and, for me, garlic is the most deserving.
—LEO BUSCAGLIA, AUTHOR

After Anita and Louie gave us the full tour of the two garlic drying barns, they took us inside the new high houses where tomatoes were growing and garlic was curing, walked us along the fields of popcorn and regular corn, explained asparagus, paraded us by the peppers, pulled some radishes out of the ground, and sent us home with some of everything!

What could someone like me offer in return to Louie and Anita for giving me so much of what I desperately needed to know about garlic? The little gift was a freshly baked batch of lemon bars, but the greater gift—and one that will keep on giving—was a few bulbs of each of the hardneck garlic varieties that I received from Sonoma, California by way of Chester Aaron. Anita and Louie can now experiment with these new to Upstate New York garlic varieties: Brown Tempest, Shatili, Ukrainian Blue, and Jharoda. So if you see these varieties of garlic in and around Rochester, New York, you'll know the original story of how they got there. This is the story of bulb bearers—a great story that follows the pattern of how garlic got from place to place throughout history. And it's happening in your very own backyard!

Zak and Zyliss

It is a zany and bizarre coincidence that the top two garlic tools are produced by companies whose names start with the letter Z.

Zak Designs sells the E-Z-Rol garlic peeler and Zyliss offers two super-impressive garlic presses. Learn more about them under *Kitchen Tools* and you'll discover what the E-Z-Rol designer played around with before he invented the E-Z-Rol. You can also visit *www.zak.com* and *www.zylissusa.com* for details or purchase these gadgets direct from *www.amazon.com* or from your favorite local cookware shop or gourmet grocery store.

CHAPTER 6

GARLIC GETAWAYS AND ESSENTIAL RESOURCES

When I agreed to write *A Miscellany of Garlic*, little did I know that it would prove to be such a discovery-filled journey. It was both a challenging research and writing project and an educational adventure filled with opportunities to meet some very remarkable people along the way—a garlic odyssey, dare I say?

A handful of exceptional people were key resources in preparing this book. They are mentioned throughout and are highlighted here. They are available as resources to you, too.

Chester Aaron

Chester is a not only an expert when it comes to garlic, he is a prolific author of many novels, stories, and memoirs, including the memoir *Garlic Is Life*. Chester was born in 1923 in a Pennsylvania coal-mining town, saw combat in World War II, and was with the troops that liberated Dachau. Following publication of his first novel in 1967, he was an X-ray technician at Alta Bates Hospital in Berkeley, California. Chester joined the faculty of Saint Mary's College in Moraga, California, and he retired as a full professor in 1997. Over the last twenty-five years, he has become known worldwide for the ninety varieties of exotic garlic he grows on his farm in Sonoma County, California, and has become a leading expert on garlic tasting. Visit him at *www.chesteraaron.com*—he is truly a kind, insightful, and inspirational guy—and his love of garlic can't help but rub off on you.

Bob Anderson and Gourmet Garlic Gardens

Bob Anderson is personally responsible for hooking me up with the good stuff, thanks to Gourmet Garlic Gardens *www.gourmetgarlicgardens.com* and his pioneering, online farmers' market initiative. The online farmers' market is a new concept that has been working out well for garlic growers and customers. Anderson describes it as a "true grassroots, or rather garlic-roots, entrepreneurial effort." The Gourmet Garlic Gardens website gives small growers a national stage on which to showcase their pride-and-joy plants without having to spend a lot of their own resources and time trying to get high visibility online. Gourmet Garlic Gardens has made ordering from independent garlic growers easy. The hard part is deciding which varieties of garlic you'd like receive in your home delivery. Bob said it himself, "They're all different and you're in for treat, after treat, after treat!"

Alley Swiss and Filaree Garlic Farm

Filaree was one of the first organic garlic farms and is a name that crops up when you start doing garlic research. The farm was started by garlic great Ron L. Engeland, author of *Growing Great Garlic*, and it is now owned by Alley Swiss. Filaree Garlic Farm has been an independently owned grower and supplier of premium quality garlic seed for thirty years. It is the largest privately held collection of garlic in North America and collects, preserves, and provides gardeners with the opportunity to grow more than 100 varieties of garlic. It serves organic gardeners, plant nurseries, and small-scale commercial growers. If you're inspired to grow your own or want to dig deeper into garlic, visit Filaree Garlic Farm online at *www.filareefarm.com*. Pick up some garlic to grow and a copy of Ron Engeland's book *Growing Great Garlic* to get started. You'll never settle for the store-bought stuff again.

Three Important Books

Three publications served as key references in compiling the information in this book, and if serious garlic is in your future, you'll want to get to know the works of Eric Block, Ron L. Engeland, and Ted Jordan Meredith, too. These guys are *the* garlic gurus and have devoted the greater parts of their lives to garlic. They've also, thankfully, put their knowledge into print to share with the rest of us. Consider adding these books to your personal library:

- *Growing Great Garlic: The Definitive Guide for Organic Gardeners and Small Farmers*, by Ron L. Engeland
- *Garlic and Other Alliums: The Lore and the Science*, by Eric Block, PhD
- *The Complete Book of Garlic: A Guide for Gardeners, Growers, and Serious Cooks*, by Ted Jordan Meredith

Online Garlic-Specific Resources

Following these links will help you get started as you begin to explore, first-hand, the wonders of great garlic right at home in your kitchen, medicine chest, or in your family's very own backyard.

Ashley Creek Farm
Olympia, Washington
www.ashleycreek.com

Bobba-Mike's Garlic Farm
Orrville, Ohio
www.garlicfarm.com

Boundary Garlic Farm
Midway, British Columbia, Canada
www.garlicfarm.ca

Cayuga Garlic Farms
Scipio Center, New York
www.cayugagarlic.com

Christopher Ranch
Gilroy, California
www.christopherranch.com

Filaree Garlic Farm
Okanogan, Washington
www.filareefarm.com

Freeman Farms
Rice, Washington
www.freemanfarms.biz

Garlic Central
www.garlic-central.com

Garlic Festival Foods
Gilroy, California
www.garlicfestival.com

Garlic Gourmay
Ariel, Washington
www.garlicgourmay.com

The Garlic Seed Foundation
Rose, New York
www.garlicseedfoundation.info

The Garlic Shoppe

Gilroy, California

www.garlicdude.com

The Garlic Store

Fort Collins, Colorado

www.thegarlicstore.com

Garlic Valley Farms

Glendale, California

www.garlicvalleyfarms.com

Garlic World

Gilroy, California

www.garlicworld.com

Gourmet Garlic Gardens

Bangs, Texas

www.gourmetgarlicgardens.com

Grey Duck Garlic

Colfax, Washington

www.greyduckgarlic.com

Hood River Garlic

Hood River, Oregon

www.hoodrivergarlic.com

Italian Rose Gourmet Products, Inc.

Riviera Beach, Florida

www.italian-rose.com

Local Harvest

Santa Cruz, California

www.localharvest.org

Montana Gourmet Garlic

Stevensville, Montana

www.montanagourmetgarlic.com

Snakeroot Organic Farm

Pittsfield, Maine

www.snakeroot.net/farm

Troy Bogdan's Pure Earth Organic Farm

Cambridge Springs, Pennsylvania

www.pureearthorganic.com

Wakunaga Nutritional Supplements/Wakunaga of America

Aged garlic extract nutritional supplements

www.kyolic.com

Restaurants Known for Great Garlic Cuisine

There are many more restaurants serving up great garlic fare, but here are a few garlic-centric restaurants that came to our attention as we did our research for this book:

The Stinking Rose

325 Columbus Avenue

San Francisco, CA 94133

Tel: 415-781-7673

www.thestinkingrose.com

The Stinking Rose

55 North La Cienega Boulevard

Beverly Hills, CA 90211

Tel: 310-652-7673

www.thestinkingrose.com

The Stinking Rose restaurants season their garlic with food.

Chez Panisse Restaurant and Café

1517 Shattuck Avenue

Berkeley, CA 94709-1516

Restaurant Tel: 510-548-5525

Café Tel: 510–548-5049

www.chezpanisse.com

Home of the first garlic festival, owned by Alice Waters, featured in the movie *Garlic Is as Good as Ten Mothers*.

Saleem's

14560 Manchester Road
Winchester, MO 63011
Tel: 636–207-1368
www.saleemswest.com
Lebanese cuisine where garlic is king.

Annual Garlic Festivals and Events

Garlic is globally revered and honored with annual celebrations worldwide. Take a break and embark upon a garlic-focused expedition with a day trip to a nearby garlic festival. Or indulge yourself with a transcontinental plane ride to explore the "stinking rose" afar—you just might fall in love abroad all over again!

Whether you're a vacationer or a "stay-cationer" these days, the information provided here will serve as a starting point for unusual, educational, and tasty travels.

Garlic Festivals in the United States

Arizona

Triangle T Annual Garlic Festival and Benefit

Dragoon, Arizona
Takes place: Late July
www.azretreatcenter.com

California

The Gilroy Garlic Festival

Gilroy, California

Takes place: The last weekend in July

www.gilroygarlicfestival.com

The original, garlic lover's Mecca and three-day eating extravaganza.

Connecticut

Garlic and Harvest Festival

Bethlehem, Connecticut

Takes place: Early October

www.garlicfestct.com

The Olde Mistick Village Garlic Festival

Mystic, Connecticut

Takes place: Mid-September

www.oldemistickvillage.com

Florida

Delray Beach Garlic Fest

Delray Beach, Florida

Takes place: Mid-February

www.dbgarlicfest.com

Maine

MDI Garlic Festival

Bar Harbor, Maine

Takes place: Mid-September

www.nostrano.com/garlic.html

Massachusetts

North Quabbin Garlic & Arts Festival

Orange, Massachusetts

Takes place: Early October

www.garlicandarts.org

Minnesota

Minnesota Garlic Festival

Hutchinson, Minnesota

Takes place: Mid-August

www.mngarlicfest.com

New Jersey

Annual Garden State Garlic Gathering

Lafayette, New Jersey

Takes place: Early October

www.garliconline.com

Annual Garlic Festival

Hoboken, New Jersey
Takes place: Mid-October
www.garliconline.com

New Mexico

¡Sostenga! Garlic Fest

Española, New Mexico
Takes place: Early July
www.nnmc.edu/gallery/sostenga
(Sponsored by the Northern New Mexico College Center for
Sustainable Foods)

New York

Cuba Garlic Festival

Cuba, New York
Takes place: Mid-September
www.cubagarlicfestival.com

Glorious Garlic Festival

Penn Yan, New York
Takes place: Early August
www.foxrunvineyards.com

Hudson Valley Garlic Festival

Saugerties, New York

Takes place: Late September

www.hudsonvalleygarlic.com

Long Island Garlic Festival

Riverhead, New York

Takes place: Late September

www.gardenofevefarm.com/garlic-festival.htm

Mohawk Valley Garlic and Herb Festival

Little Falls, New York

Takes place: Mid-September

www.mvghf.com

Ohio

Cleveland Garlic Festival

Cleveland, Ohio

Takes place: Mid-September

www.clevelandgarlicfestival.org

Oregon

Elephant Garlic Festival

North Plains, Oregon

Takes place: Mid-August

www.funstinks.com

(Included here even though elephant garlic is really a leek.)

Pennsylvania

Easton Garlic Fest

Easton, Pennsylvania

Takes place: Late September or early October

www.eastongarlicfest.com

(Eat, Drink, and Stink)

Keystone State Hot and Stinky Garlic and Herb Festival

Drums, Pennsylvania

Takes place: Late August

www.zanolininursery.com/Garlicfestivals.ivnu

Pocono Garlic Festival

At Shawnee Mountain in East Stroudsburg, PA

Takes place: Early September

www.poconogarlic.com

Red, Ripe & Roasted: Tomato & Garlic Festival

Phipps Conservatory and Botanical Gardens

Pittsburgh, Pennsylvania

Takes place: Late August

http://phipps.conservatory.org

Vermont

Southern Vermont Garlic and Herb Festival

Bennington, Vermont

Takes place: Early September

www.lovegarlic.com

Virginia

Stoney Lonesome Garlic Festival

Gainesville, Virginia

Takes place: Late June

www.slfarm.us

Virginia Wine and Garlic Festival

Rebec Vineyards, Amherst, Virginia

Takes place: Early October

www.rebecwinery.com

Washington State

Annual Garlic Festival at Northwest Organic Farms

Ridgefield, Washington

Takes place: Mid-September

www.northwestorganicfarms.com/annual-garlic-festival

Chehalis Annual Garlic Festival and Craft Show

Chehalis, Washington

Takes place: Late August

www.chehalisgarlicfest.com

China Bend Winery Annual Garlic Faire

Kettle Falls, Washington

Takes place: Mid- to late August

www.chinabend.com

Northwest Garlic Festival

Ocean Park, Washington

Takes place: Mid-June

www.opwa.com (Look under Ocean Park Events)

Tonasket Garlic Festival

Tonasket, Washington

Takes place: Late August

www.communityculturalcenter.org/Garlic_Festival.php

Garlic Festivals in Canada

Sorrentino's Garlic Festival

Edmonton and St. Albert, Alberta

Takes place: Events are held in March and April

www.sorrentinos.com

Grindrod Garlic Festival

Grindrod, British Columbia

Takes place: Mid- to late August

www.greencroftgardens.com/garlicfest.html

Hills Garlic Festival

New Denver, British Columbia

Takes place: Early to mid-September

www.hillsgarlicfest.ca

Pender Harbour Garlic Festival

Pender Harbour, British Columbia

Takes place: Mid- to late August

www.penderharbourgarlicfestival.ca

South Cariboo Garlic Festival

Lac La Hache, British Columbia

Takes place: Late August

www.garlicfestival.ca

Carp Farmers' Market Garlic Festival

Carp, Ontario

Takes place: Mid-August

www.carpfarmersmarket.com

Perth Lions Garlic Festival

Perth, Ontario

Takes place: Mid-August

www.perthgarlicfestival.com

Stratford Garlic Festival

Stratford, Ontario

Takes place: Early to mid-September

www.stratfordgarlicfestival.com

Toronto Garlic Festival

Toronto, Ontario

Takes place: Late September

www.torontogarlicfestival.ca

Verona Lions Garlic Festival

Verona, Ontario

Takes place: Early September

www.frontenacfarmersmarket.ca

Garlic Festivals Abroad

France

Fête de l'ail de Cherrueix

Cherrueix, France

Takes place: End of July

www.fetedelail.fr

Fête de l'ail Rose de Lautrec

Lautrec, France

Takes place: Early August

www.ailrosedelautrec.com

La Foire à l'ail Fumé

Arleux, France
Takes place: Early September
www.arleux.fr/foire-a-lail-fume
(Pink garlic competition)

Italy

L'Aglio di Voghiera

Voghiera, Ferrara, Italy
Takes place: Early August
www.agliodivoghiera.com

Turkey

International Culture, Garlic and Flex Festival

Taşköprü, Kastamonu, Turkey
Takes place: Early to mid-September
www.turkeycentral.com/kastamonu/index.php

United Kingdom

The Isle of Wight Garlic Festival

Sandown, Isle of Wight
Takes place: Mid- to late August
www.garlic-festival.co.uk

BIBLIOGRAPHY AND REFERENCES

GENERAL GARLIC AND ALLIUM GUIDES, HANDBOOKS, AND VIDEOTAPES

Block, Eric. *Garlic and Other Alliums: The Lore and the Science.* Cambridge, UK: The Royal Society of Chemistry, 2010.

Garlic's Pungent Presence. Norwood, MA: Beacon Films Magic Lantern Production, 1985.

Harris, Lloyd J. *The Book of Garlic.* Berkeley, CA: Aris Books/Harris Publishing Company, Inc., 1983.

Harris, Lloyd J. *The Official Garlic Lovers Handbook.* Berkeley, CA: Aris Books/Harris Publishing Company, Inc., 1986.

Hughes, Meredith Sayles. *Stinky and Stringy: Stem & Bulb Vegetables.* Minneapolis, MN: Lerner Publications Company, 1998.

Meredith, Ted Jordan. *The Complete Book of Garlic: A Guide for Gardeners, Growers, and Serious Cooks.* Portland, OR: Timber Press, Inc., 2008.

Moyers, Susan. *Garlic in Health, History, and World Cuisine.* St. Petersburg, FL: Suncoast Press, 1996.

Platt, Ellen Spector. *Garlic, Onion, & Other Alliums.* Mechanicsburg, PA: Stackpole Books, 2003.

Renoux, Victoria. *For the Love of Garlic: The Complete Guide to Garlic Cuisine.* Garden City Park, NY: Square One Publishers, 2005.

COOKING AND KITCHEN REFERENCES

Adam, Cornelia. *Garlic.* San Francisco, CA: Silverback Books, Inc., 2001.

Baker, Sunny and Michelle Sbraga. *The Unabashed Onion & Garlic Lover's International Cookbook.* Garden City Park, NY: Avery Publishing Group, 1995.

Batcheller, Barbara. *The Lilies of the Kitchen: Recipes Celebrating Onions, Garlic, Leeks, Shallots, Scallions, and Chives.* New York, NY: St. Martin's Press, 1986.

Belsinger, Susan and Carolyn Dille. *The Garlic Book: A Garland of Simple, Savory, Robust Recipes.* Loveland, CO: Interweave Press, Inc., 1993.

Capalbo, Carla, Kate Whiteman, Jeni Wright, and Angela Boggiano. *The Italian Cooking Encyclopedia.* London, England: Anness Publishing Limited, 2001.

Fox, Margaret S. and John Bear. *Café Beaujolais.* Berkeley, CA: Ten Speed Press, 1984.

Froncillo, Andrea and Jennifer Jeffrey. *The Stinking Rose Restaurant Cookbook.* Berkeley, CA: Ten Speed Press, 2006.

Gilroy Garlic Festival Staff. *The Complete Garlic Lovers Cookbook.* Berkeley, CA: Celestial Arts, 1987.

Griffith, Linda and Fred Griffith. *Garlic, Garlic, Garlic: More Than 200 Exceptional Recipes for the World's Most Indispensable Ingredient.* New York, NY: Houghton Mifflin Company, 1998.

Herbst, Sharon Tyler. *The New Food Lover's Companion: Comprehensive Definitions of over 3000 Food, Wine, and Culinary Terms.* Hauppauge, NY: Barron's Educational Series, 1995.

Roberts-Dominguez, Jan. *The Onion Book.* New York, NY: Doubleday, 1996.

Rombauer, Irma S. and Marion Rombauer Becker. *Joy of Cooking.* Indianapolis, IN: Plume, 1973.

GARDENING AND HERBS

Coonse, Marian. *Onions, Leeks, & Garlic: A Handbook for Gardeners.* College Station, TX: Texas A&M University Press, 1995.

Crockett, James Underwood and Ogden Tanner. *Herbs.* Alexandria VA: Time-Life Books, 1977.

Engeland, Ron L. *Growing Great Garlic: The Definitive Guide for Organic Gardeners and Small Farmers.* Okanogan, WA: Filaree Productions, 1991.

Jones, Louisa. *Gardens in Provence.* Paris, France: Flammarion, 2001.

Mindell, Earl. *Earl Mindell's Herb Bible.* New York, NY: Simon & Schuster/ Fireside, 1992.

Riotte, Louise. *Roses Love Garlic: Companion Planting and Other Secrets of Flowers.* North Adams, MA: Storey Publishing, 1998.

Rose, Jeanne. *Herbs & Things.* New York, NY: The Putnam Publishing Group, 1983.

Schwartz, Howard F. and S. Krishna Mohan, ed. *Compendium of Onion and Garlic Diseases and Pests.* St. Paul, MN: APS Press/The American Phytopatholocial Society, 1995.

HEALTH, HEALING, AND MEDICINE

Adams, Rex. *Miracle Medicine Foods.* New York, NY: Warner Books, 1977.

Aggarwal, Bharat B., PhD and Debora Yost. *Healing Spices: How to Use 50 Everyday and Exotic Spices to Boost Health and Beat Disease.* New York, NY: Sterling Publishing Co., Inc., 2011.

Bergner, Paul. *Healing Power of Garlic: The Enlightened Person's Guide to Nature's Most Versatile Medicinal Plant.* Rocklin, CA: Prima Publishing, 1996.

Caduto, Michael J. *Everyday Herbs in Spiritual Life: A Guide to Many Practices.* Woodstock, VT: SkyLight Paths Publishing, 2007.

Fulder, Stephen PhD and John Blackwood. *Garlic: Nature's Original Remedy.* Rochester, VT: Healing Arts Press, 2000.

Heinerman, John PhD. *The Healing Benefits of Garlic.* New Canaan, CT: Keats Publishing, Inc. 1994.

Ingels, Darin. *Natural Treatments for High Cholesterol.* Roseville, CA: Prima Publishing, 2000.

Kato, Yoshio. *Garlic: The Unknown Miracle Worker—Odorless garlic medicine and garlic Flow-Leben.* Amagasaki, Japan: Oyama Garlic Laboratory, 1973.

Lau, Benjamin, MD, PhD. *Garlic for Health.* Wilmot, WI: Lotus Light Publications, 1988.

McKeith, Gillian. *Gillian McKeith's Food Bible: How to Use Food to Cure What Ails You.* New York, NY: Plume/Penguin Group, 2009.

O'Brien, James Edmond. *The Miracle of Garlic & Vinegar.* Boca Raton, FL: Globe Communications Corp., 1999.

Prevention Magazine Editors and William P. Castelli. *Cholesterol Cures: More Than 325 Natural Ways to Lower Cholesterol and Live Longer.* Prevention Health Books/Rodale, Inc., 2002.

Quillin, Patrick. *Honey, Garlic & Vinegar: Home Remedies and Recipes.* North Canton, OH: The Leader Co, Inc., 1996.

Wilen, Joan and Lydia Wilen. *Garlic: Nature's Super Healer.* Paramus, NJ: Prentice Hall, 1997.

HISTORY, CULTURE, AND RELIGION

Crawford, Stanley. *A Garlic Testament: Seasons on a Small New Mexico Farm.* New York, NY: HarperCollins Publishers, Inc., 1998.

Greenspoon, Leonard J., Ronald A. Simkins, and Gerald Shapiro, eds. *Food & Judaism.* Omaha, NE: Creighton University Press, 2005.

Helstosky, Carol F. *Garlic & Oil: Food and Politics in Italy.* Oxford, UK: Berg, 2006.

Hull, Edward. *The Wall Chart of World History.* London: Bracken Books, 1989.

INDEX